MW00998077

SCRATCH
THAT

ALIX TRAEGER

SCRATCH THAT

Embrace the Mess, Cook to Impress

Photographs by Kristin Teig

UNION SQUARE & CO.

NEW YORK

UNION
SQUARE
& CO.
NEW YORK

For information about custom editions,
special sales, and premium purchases,
please contact specialsales@
unionsquareandco.com.

Printed in China

10 9 8 7 6 5 4 3 2 1

unionsquareandco.com

Editor: Amanda Englander
Designer: Renée Bollier
Photographer: Kristin Teig
Food Stylist: Marian Cooper Cairns
Prop Stylist: Jacklyn Kershek
Project Editor: Ivy McFadden
Production Manager: Kevin Iwano

Additional image credits:
Page 139: Nathan Ng
Throughout: Shutterstock.com:
   Rolau Elena (endpapers);
   Oleksandr Poliashenko (arrows);
   Polina Tomtosova (doodles and
   underlines)

To Mom & Dad,
for loving me into myself

To Z,
for loving me as myself

To all of my past versions,
and to all of yours, too

CONTENTS

IT'S BEEN A LONG TIME COMING...

My name is Alix Traeger, I'm your favorite chef's favorite mess, and if I can write a book, you can do ANYTHING—literally anything.

I hate to kick off with such a cliché, but really, I never thought I had this in me. I'm not a particularly patient person; I have the memory of a goldfish and the attention span of, well, a millennial. The highest grade I ever received on a written assignment beyond middle school was probably a B, and I always wrote my essays the night before they were due. I was definitely a better procrastinator than I was a student. Alas, the extent of my writing these days is mostly packaged into an Instagram caption, but if you're reading this right now, well, that means I did it. I freaking did it. (Also, did I really just use the word "alas"? How author of me.) What I'm trying to say is, whatever idea you're sitting on top of, whatever dreams you've kept locked up tight in your brain or your heart, whatever hobbies you've thrown in the towel on, take this book as your sign that it's never too late. In fact, I find the timing is always perfect. Take it from me: I wrote this cookbook when I was single, sold it when I had a girlfriend, and now that it's in your hand, I've got a ring on mine. So yeah, it's been a long time coming. Some may say I'm late to the game, but I choose to believe I'm right on time. I'm showing up now with every bit of preparedness and perspective I've learned throughout my life so far.

About Me

If you're here, it's likely you've seen my videos and know me as the clumsy, loud, messy girl who should never have been allowed in the kitchen to begin with. I'm here to tell you that is exactly who I am. But I didn't wait to be allowed in the kitchen. Instead, I made my place there. People often think I fake spilling things, that I do it on purpose for views and laughs, but I can assure you, I'm not that strategic. While some people have a green thumb, I have butterfingers. Spilling is a skill—a sport, if you will—but it's not one that has ever—and I mean EVER—deterred me from pursuing a career in cooking. Instead, I've leaned straight into my clumsy nature. I show my messes and my failures because they're *real*. Real for me, and I know for many others. It's a part of the cooking process, and growing up, I didn't see enough of it.

As a kid, instead of cartoons, I watched the Food Network. I idolized Julia, Ina, Rachael, Emeril, and Martha. I would even pretend I had my own cooking show while I helped my mom in the kitchen, narrating every step with my best "TV voice." The only issue was that I could never do it as gracefully as my TV chef idols could. I made mistakes, while they could make a perfect three-course dinner in the span of a thirty-minute show without breaking a sweat. But I kept stumbling clumsily forward, cooking in my kitchen when I was still in school, which led me to start a food blog, which led me to working as a food stylist in Sweden after college, which led me to Tasty, where you may know me from. It wasn't until those many years later, making and—this is the key part—editing my own food videos that it hit me: Those "perfect" TV chefs *all* made mistakes. They all spilled, and burned, and dropped things—we just weren't seeing it. And so through my entire career, I've made it my mission to share as authentically as possible, both in and out of the kitchen. Because believe me, I'm not a mess just in the kitchen. This book, just like my videos, includes the successes *and* the failures. While you can learn a lot from the successes, I wholeheartedly believe you can learn even more from the mistakes. It's kind of my whole life philosophy.

As humans, we tend to hang on to beliefs about who we are that make up our identities, and one day something happens to bring it all crumbling down. Just look at me: I used to be straight and a Tasty producer; now I'm gay and self-employed. At some point, you're left with no choice but to say, "Scratch that." To start *again* from scratch, to redefine yourself, or, better yet, to start living life beyond any definition. A key part of the journey is letting things burn, whether those things are

cakes or identities. Cooking, like any creative process, can help teach us who we are. Believe it or not, this book was originally titled *Hot Mess*, and it had been years in the making when, for reasons I won't bore you with, we had to say *Scratch That*. (See what I did there?) Having to quickly pivot on my title was equal parts frustrating and frightening. My whole being was wrapped up in that idea of "The Hot Mess," and for a split second, I felt like all my hard work had been for nothing. But I choose to frame every challenge as an opportunity for growth, and this one was no different. I can proudly pass on the title of *Hot Mess*, knowing full well that you can take the hot mess out of the title but you can't take the hot mess out of the book. Some days you're going to spend hours in the kitchen only to say *Scratch That* when the cookie crumbles. But that doesn't mean that time was a waste—instead, just use those cookie crumbs to fill and top your cake. And the next time you bake, you'll have one more data point to make you a better cook.

How to Use This Book

The intention of this book is not to teach you how to cook, nor is it to teach you how to live, since I'm definitely still learning how to do both. If you've ever accidentally added salt instead of sugar or stood under your smoke detector fanning it to stop the beeping, this cookbook is for you. Sometimes all you can do is roll with the punches, laugh it off, and learn as you go. That's what this cookbook is all about: letting our messes and mistakes guide us in the kitchen, just as previous versions of ourselves guide us to new and improved ones. Just like flour, we all (have a) purpose; I think of my purpose as much more of a philosophy than a skill. I want to encourage others to lighten up, accept their mistakes as part of the journey, and find a way to laugh through the process, all while eating food that tastes *good*.

I developed these recipes to be full of the flavor and fun you may already know me for. They're designed to be approachable yet stretch your skills in the kitchen and help inspire you to find your own creative cooking flair. The best gift I can give you is to help you turn up the voice of your own intuition: That voice is like a recipe ready to guide you—you just need to tap into it. My goal is to help you learn to trust the process and to keep going even when things go wrong. We're embracing the chaos of cooking and building confidence in the same way we build flavor.

We put way too much pressure on ourselves to perform, to be perfect. You don't have to show up perfectly, but you *do* have to show up. So as you make your way through these 102 recipes, I give you permission to breathe, to laugh, to cry, and, most important, to take the pressure off. I've peppered in little nuggets of wisdom that have helped make my journey in and out of the kitchen a little smoother. Truthfully, my life has been about as smooth as crunchy peanut butter—but crunchy peanut butter happens to be my favorite kind. Check out the "Hot Tips" throughout to learn how to turn messes into successes in the kitchen. And if you make a mistake that just can't be salvaged, just say scratch that and try again another time.

This cookbook is organized into chapters (I know, how revolutionary) based on how I personally like to cook and eat. My breakfast on a weekday consists of a

When it comes to cooking, most people will tell you to follow the rules. I will tell you to be bold enough to break them.

You know how we all have an inner child? I also believe we all have an inner chef, and that the two are intertwined, because what it takes to be an incredible chef is the spirit of a child. Pure creative genius, no blocks or barriers, no rules, no second-guessing. Healing your inner child is the most important work you can do in this life: It will clear the path to all your hopes and dreams, it will bring your passions to light, and it's what will guide you to excellence in your field, whether that be the kitchen or outer space. Children see the world with curiosity and wonder. They experiment, and regardless of whether they feel ill-equipped, they play. That's what cooking is to me: a playground. A chance to use your hands, get messy, create, learn, and savor life. Heal your inner child and unlock your inner chef.

double cappuccino and maybe a banana if I'm feeling frisky, so I kicked things off with Weekend Breakfast, where the mornings are slow, the vibes are high, and Sundays are not so scary. Next up is Salads, Soups & Sandys, which, in my opinion, are the quintessential lunch foods, but please feel free to eat these for dinner if you choose. Then Dips, Snacks & Apps—think all things predinner and/or girl dinner/snacky dinner/ whatever we're calling it these days. Then we get into the dinner mains, which have a food for every mood, I promise. I've also included a whole chapter on Sides, because we all know that sides are the best and deserve a main place. And to wrap it all up: Sweet Treats, because we save the best for last in this house. While the recipes in this book are varied, I can boil each one down to three words: approachable, playful, and comforting. I want you to feel inspired and invited into the kitchen to make them, and I've poured my heart, and soul, and stomach into each and every recipe with the hope that you love and savor them as much as I do!

Scratch That is a cookbook, but I want it to be more than that. I want it to be your journal, your best friend, your safe place, your totally judgment-free zone that also happens to be full of food you can eat all day, every day. For me, the kitchen has always been my haven; cooking has been my therapy. As much as I love to eat, the joy of cooking is not only about the food, it's about the journey. The oopsies, whoopsies, and oh-shits are those pivotal moments that will guide the way.

In my twenty-five years of cooking, or at least of eating, I've learned that even the best recipes aren't foolproof. It seems so obvious, yet no one ever says it out loud: Cooking takes practice. But just like writing a book, ANYONE can do it. You just need to turn off the pressure to be perfect, have a little more fun, and START. Start slow and steady if that feels good, or fast and chaotic if that's more your vibe. I'm not here to judge. The best cooking equipment for you is whatever you have in your kitchen right now. Seriously. This may be very controversial, but I believe there are no rules, no wrong way to cook or to live. At the end of the day, it's going in *your* mouth, so do it your way.

Cooking is massively intuitive. I probably shouldn't admit this in my own cookbook, but I don't typically use recipes. I prefer to live life on a whim and go with the flow. I use recipes like I use bumper lanes in bowling: to gently guide me to that strike. Cooking usually doesn't need to be precise, and flavors are so personal and subjective. So I give you written permission (here it is, in print!) to make whatever changes you like to any of these recipes to make them your own. Kick up the spice if you dare, switch up the flavors if you want. Don't use mayonnaise if it freaks you out. Just please, for the love of god, trust in your own ability to make a kick-ass meal for yourself.

You don't have to be a chef to cook, you don't have to be a writer to write, you don't have to be a dancer to dance. I'm not any of these things, but cooking, writing, and dancing are some of my favorite things to do. What a loss it would be if I didn't do them because I didn't feel like I was good enough. I'm not the best at anything, and accepting that is my superpower. I find that most of the time when I don't like doing something, it's because I'm trying to be something I'm not—that takes the fun out of it. I hesitated to write a book because I didn't feel like I had anything pro-found to say or enough life experience yet to make an impact with my words. But not everything we do has to change the world. You don't have to make a dish wor-thy of a Michelin star for it to be great, and I happen to love a five-minute mug cake on nights I'm feeling lazy and tired. Sure, I would love more than anything to change even one person's life with my writing, but if I don't, at least you got some good food out of it. To me, that's enough.

I'm a very (very) open person. An oversharer, if you will. I've made sharing my life my career. I think this book is the one thing in my life I've kept very close to me. I can make a cooking video in one day, but this book took me years to write. Well, here it is—finally. I hope as you read it and cook from it, and likely spill all over it, you become a better cook, and maybe even a better version of yourself. Not a day goes by that I am not grateful to be in your home, in your kitchen, and hopefully in your heart. Thank you, from my stomach to yours, for trusting me with that honor.

23 MY MANTRAS

1 HAVE MORE FUN

2 LEARN AS YOU GO

3 MOVE TOWARD THE HARD THINGS

MESS EN PLACE

THE MAGIC OF THE MESS

I believe *The Mess* is an integral part of every creative process. In cooking, *mise en place* is French for "everything in its place"—every ingredient is measured, chopped, and ready to go before you even turn on the stove. Pardon my French, but the best dishes aren't only born in spotless kitchens—they're also crafted in the whirlwind of flour clouds, splattered sauces, and the occasional stray herb, because The Mess is where we learn.

Mess en Place is my version; it means "let's get real." It's about prepping your space for an inevitable mess and finding the joy in the journey, not just the destination. While we're here to embrace The Mess, a little organization goes a long way to ensure your final dish is delicious, not disastrous.

Calm Before the Storm

Lay out your ingredients, but unless you're baking, don't stress about perfectly measured quantities. Cooking is about feeling as much as it is about following the rules. Prepare your tools, and consider a cute apron to collect those glorious splatters.

Controlled Chaos

Create a clean space for chaos—aka controlled chaos. Start with a tidy workspace so that as the mess grows, you don't get overwhelmed and still know where everything is . . . kind of.

No-Stress Mess

Remember, the mess is part of the process. Each splatter, spill, burn, and smear is one step closer to making magic.

RECIPE FOR SUCCESS

Cooking is an art and a skill that develops over time with practice. It's about the process, not the destination, but sometimes we can help each other get there a little faster. These are the most important lessons I've learned in my own culinary adventure.

Taste as You Go

It's always easier to make corrections during the cooking process rather than after the dish is complete, so taste your food as it cooks! Tasting along the way allows you to adjust seasoning and build flavors as you go, resulting in a balanced, well-seasoned, and deliciously complex dish. It's also how you'll learn which flavors specific ingredients add.

Knife Skills Matter

A good chef's knife is arguably your most important tool. This may sound counterintuitive, but the sharper your knife is, the safer it is to use—plus, uniformly cut ingredients cook more evenly. Let's practice! Grab your chef's knife and wrap your fingers around the handle, firmly but not overly tight. Don't leave your pointer finger on top of the blade! Cut in a rocking motion: The tip of the knife should stay in contact with the cutting board while you push down toward the heel of the blade. Use your free hand to hold the food securely, keeping your fingertips tucked under like a claw and your knuckles parallel to the knife as a guide to prevent accidents. Okay, chop chop!

Patience Is a Virtue

Many dishes require time to develop flavor. Rushing through cooking can lead to undercooked or unevenly cooked food. Practice patience in life, and especially when simmering, roasting, braising, caramelizing, and marinating. Use the cues and times I've provided in the recipes as guidance.

Climate Control

Staying in control of your cooking temp is key! Whether you're sautéing with a *sizzle*, simmering with a soft *bubble*, or baking to a golden *crisp*, each heat level has its own outcome. Trust your gut—and your senses! If you hear a *crackle* turning into a *smoky whiff* or see edges browning too fast, dial it down. If it's quieter than a library and smells like, well, nothing, crank it up!

Make It Work

Learning to substitute ingredients and adapt recipes to your taste is an invaluable skill. Don't be afraid to make swaps—you just might make a recipe even better! Start simple, like choosing one green for another or throwing in the herbs you have on hand rather than going out to buy what's called for. Get those creative juices flowing; experimentation is how you develop your personal style. Sometimes a swap will be a flop, but that's okay, because you miss 100% of the recipes you don't make.

Master Disaster

Not to sound like a broken record, but this *is* my life's purpose. At this point I'm a master of disaster, but everyone makes mistakes (everybody has those days). Burned something? Oversalted a dish? Forgot to add an ingredient? View those moments as opportunities to learn. Embrace your mistakes! After all, the *worse* you burn something, the *more* it's burned into your brain.

THE SCRATCH THAT PANTRY

Pantries are personal. What kind of pasta to buy (*cough* RIGATONI), or which agents of heat to have in your arsenal—that's up to your palate! Keeping a stocked pantry is a helpful cooking tool when you need to adjust and correct flavors in case you accidentally make a mistake (which by now you have hopefully accepted is *definitely* going to happen). Here's what I keep on hand.

Salt: The OG. Salt enhances flavor—it's what makes good food great.

Acid: When things get too salty, fatty, sweet, bitter, or spicy, acid adds a pop of zing to keep everything in balance; try a splash of vinegar or a squeeze of citrus juice like lemon or lime.

Sugar: Not just for desserts, give your dish a little sweet lovin' when too-spicy, too-bitter, or too-acidic notes take over. White granulated sugar is a classic but you can also play with brown sugar, honey, or maple syrup for a little more oomph.

Low-sodium stock or broth: Maximize your stock options for a rainy day (in this case rain = salt). Use it to dilute oversalted soups, stews, and sauces while adding just a touch of flavor.

Potatoes: Think of spuds as sponges. If you have oversalted soup or stew, throw in some cut-up raw potatoes and let them soak up the saltiness. You can discard them once they've done their job.

Plain yogurt or sour cream: Creamy, tangy, and the secret to cooling down dishes that got a little too spicy or salty.

Heavy cream or milk: A dairy option that adds a luscious richness to reduce spiciness or saltiness without introducing the tang that yogurt or sour cream adds.

Baking soda: I have baking soda . . . to cut through a too-sour or too-acidic dish. A little goes a long way—too much and things start to taste . . . off.

Butter: Typically responsible for the "I can't stop eating this" effect. And brown butter? Even *better* butter.

Plain or panko breadcrumbs: Toasted with butter, salt, and maybe even a little cheese, will add texture and crunch to dishes that need a lil' something extra.

Fresh herbs: A pop of color, a burst of freshness, and bonus—they can cover up any mistake on the plate. Herbs make everything look (and taste) better.

Spices: The spice of life! Spices add flavor, color, and a touch of mystery that'll make people ask, "What's in this?! It tastes amazing!" Don't be shy—get bold and playful with them!

Cornstarch or flour: The secret (thickening) agents when sauces are runny and thin. Throw in a little cornstarch or mix equal parts melted butter and flour. Whisk well to avoid lumps.

Tomato paste: A little tomato paste can bring richness and umami, giving your food a deeper, more savory flavor.

Wine: Perfect for deglazing all those browned bits stuck to the pan, boosting flavor, and—most importantly—sipping as you cook.

Dijon mustard: The sharpness will cut through fats and bring balance to your marinades, dressings, and sauces.

Low-sodium soy sauce: Provides a boost of umami and saltiness if a dish is lackluster.

V. I. F.

VERY IMPORTANT FLAVORS

SALTY

EARTHY NUTTY

SOUR

UMAMI RICH

TANGY

SPICY

SWEET

SMOKY
CREAMY
BITTER

FATTY

What I Mean When I Say . . .

Kosher salt is used in cooking because, compared to table salt, it has larger, coarser crystals. Those crystals make it much easier to pinch, sprinkle, or throw over your shoulder and onto your food. My preferred brand of kosher salt is **DIAMOND CRYSTAL**. It's less salty than other brands, which means I get to use bigger pinches than I would with another salt. Are you starting to clock why all this matters? If all you've got is table salt or Morton kosher salt, start with half the amount listed in the recipe (if there is a measurement) and taste and adjust as you go. I encourage you to find the salt that aligns with *you* (aka your taste preferences and cooking style), and most importantly, stick to it to learn how to cook with it.

Flaky salt is made of large and, well, flaky crystals. It's best used for finishing, to add a burst of saltiness and a satisfying crunch. I usually use **MALDON**, but the brand makes less of a difference here than it does for kosher salt. You can find lots of fun flavored salts to use for finishing. Still, I typically prefer to keep it simple to let the flaky salt enhance my ingredients and make them shine rather than mask the flavors of my food (unless you need it to mask the flavor of your food—then, by all means, go ahead). Use flaky salt to finish salads, grilled vegetables, steaks, roasted meats, and especially on desserts like chocolate chip cookies.

Black pepper is always **FRESHLY GROUND**, and you can play with how fine or coarse you like to set your grinder.

Eggs are always **LARGE**. I look for pasture-raised or farm-fresh when purchasing eggs.

Citrus juice is always **FRESH** and from a whole fruit. The bottled stuff is not worth your money!

Vegetable oil is used for high-heat cooking applications and frying. I use **CANOLA** or **PEANUT OIL**. Avocado and grapeseed oils are also good options for roasting and searing.

Olive oil is not all made the same. **EXTRA-VIRGIN (EVOO)** is great for you and great for cooking. It has a lower smoke point, though, so it's not ideal for high-heat cooking. Save the pricier bottles for uncooked applications like salad dressings and drizzling over finished dishes!

Butter is **UNSALTED**, unless salted is called for specifically. That way, you can control the salt content in the food without going over(butter)board.

Stock and broth may seem interchangeable, but each has its own place in the kitchen. When I cook, I use **LOW-SODIUM STOCK**. It's made from simmering bones (sometimes with a bit of meat), making it richer thanks to all that gelatin (gnarly, I know). It's perfect for adding depth and body to soups, stews, and sauces, but leaves the salt up to you. Broth, on the other hand, is made by simmering meat (maybe a bone or two) with veg and seasonings, resulting in a lighter, flavorful liquid good for sippin' on its own. In a nutshell, you should use stock for richness and broth for a lighter touch, but really, use whatever you've got.

Dairy is **FULL-FAT** because fat = flavor! That means when a recipe calls for milk, I use whole milk. If you have dietary restrictions, feel free to use your favorite nondairy alternative. When using alternative milks, I recommend scanning the ingredient list and choosing ones with minimal additives, avoiding unnecessary preservatives or sweeteners.

Cheese is **GRATED BY YOU**. Preshredded and grated cheeses have additives and other junk that alter their flavor and prevent them from melting nicely.

Parmesan (or Parm) only means real **PARMIGIANO REGGIANO**. Look for the stamp of authenticity—it's always worth the splurge.

Herbs are always a **SUGGESTION**! Switch and swap to your liking and use what you have on hand. Just note that when I call for parsley, it's always flat-leaf, also known as Italian. The curly kind is for buffet decorations.

OOPS, I DID IT AGAIN: COMMON COOKING MISTAKES

Here's a guide to some of the most common kitchen mishaps and how to save them before you need to *Scratch That*. You can find more of these Hot Tips following each and every recipe in this book, helping you avoid some of the scenarios I find myself in all too regularly.

OOPS

THE FIX

Season with Your Soul

Your food tastes blander than cardboard.

People are generally more conservative with their use of salt than they should be, and a pinch is bigger than you think! I firmly believe food is more commonly undersalted in the cooking process than oversalted. Season with your soul and never rely on a last-minute dash of salt, you should season gradually and build each layer of your dish like a house. Seasoning along the way also requires tasting along the way—so keep a spoon nearby. By seasoning along the way, the salt will meld with each ingredient resulting in a stronger house—I mean, dish. By tasting along the way, you can monitor how the flavors change and when your food is seasoned enough. That being said, no one is ever mad about a final sprinkle of flaky salt on top.

Burn, Baby, Burn

You turned your kitchen into Burning Man.

Sometimes things burn past the point of no return, like that time at Tasty when I was making the infamous chocolate croissants. What you didn't see was that someone (accidentally) turned on the oven my final croissants were rising inside of. Let's just say it wasn't pretty. We were already two weeks deep into the shoot and I had no choice but to run to Trader Joe's to be able to finish the video. If you look closely, you'll notice that very movie-magic swap. So whether you trim off the burnt parts, salvage whatever's salvageable, or run to the store, the important thing is laughing it off and learning.

Pasta Disasta

Your pasta's gone from al dente to just plain mushy.

Drain it, rinse with cold water to stop the cooking, and toss it in your sauce. Compensate with added crunch from panko, nuts, fried onions, or crispy bacon. You may be stuck with mushy pasta this time, but remember it's always better to have extra–al dente pasta that finishes cooking in the sauce.

OOPS

THE FIX

Too Hot to Handle

Your spice level escalated from mild to mouth-numbing.

I'm a spice wimp, so this happens a lot. I've learned to balance the heat with sweetness or acidity. A dollop of honey, a splash of citrus, and/or a generous scoop of yogurt can cool things down. And hey, at the end of the day, by adding too much spice, you may just build up your spice tolerance—I've done it this very way!

Sticky Situation

Your ingredients are acting like a stage 5 clinger.

First, breathe. Next, add a bit of oil or a splash of liquid (stock, wine, water) to the pan to loosen things up. Adjust the heat, if needed. Next time, give your pan a good preheating and be sure your ingredients are dry before they hit the heat. When using stainless steel, time and temperature are critical because things release from the pan once they are cooked and ready to, not one second sooner, so you will need to practice trust and patience. Remember, *build a good sear, and you're in the clear.*

I Dough Know

Your dough is sandy as a beach or gooey as quicksand.

If it's too dry, add a bit of liquid (water or milk—whatever the main liquid in the recipe is) If it's too wet, sprinkle in some more flour. Maybe even watch some videos on proper kneading techniques. Time is your friend here—time will allow your flour to hydrate, so sometimes dough needs a moment to relax and get its act together. Don't we all?

Something's Missing

You're knee-deep in a recipe and you realize you forgot a crucial ingredient.

It's your time to shine! Sometimes being too dependent on a recipe inhibits us from building confidence in the kitchen. There is nothing more freeing than getting creative and making a recipe your own. Raid your pantry or fridge for substitutes. Missing fresh herbs? Go for dried. No stock? Water, bouillon, a splash of wine, or citrus juice all work. The kitchen is your canvas—paint with the ingredients you have.

When Life Gives You Salt, Make Lemonade

Rein it in, salt bae, you got a bit carried away.

Now acid is your BFF. Add a squeeze of lemon juice or a splash of vinegar to balance out the excess saltiness. If it's a soup or stew, throw in some extra veggies, grains, or potatoes to soak up the salt.

THE SIX COOKING SENSES

HEARING

SMELL

INTUITION

TOUCH

TASTE

SIGHT

ONE

WEEKEND BREAKFAST

Banana Pudding Banana Bread

Longtime fans might remember a time in my career when I was obsessed with bananas, and more specifically, banana-flavored things. My first Tasty video was even banana-flavored. Well, nothing has changed, and when I was brainstorming recipes for this book, it was recommended to me that I cool it on the banana. Lucky for you, this one made the cut—it was the best of the bunch. Banana bread is arguably the king of all banana-flavored things, but I believe it's about time banana pudding gets its flowers. This recipe has it all: the luxurious, creamy, banana-y goodness that is banana pudding, all wrapped up in the form of the beloved banana bread. There's a reason this is the first recipe of my first cookbook. If I am going to have a signature recipe, let it be this one. Why are you still reading this? Get cooking!

Makes one 9-inch loaf

Unsalted butter or vegetable oil, for greasing

2 cups cake flour or all-purpose flour

2 cups Nilla Wafers, crushed into pea-size pieces

1 (3.4-ounce) box instant vanilla pudding mix

1 teaspoon baking soda

1 teaspoon kosher salt

4 or 5 very ripe, very spotty, almost black bananas (use 5 if they're a little smaller or for the most banana-y flavor)

½ cup (1 stick) unsalted butter, melted and cooled

¾ cup packed light or dark brown sugar

2 large eggs, at room temperature

⅓ cup sweetened condensed milk

2 teaspoons pure vanilla extract

1   Preheat the oven to 350°F. Grease a 9 × 5-inch loaf pan.

2   In a medium bowl, whisk together the flour, crushed cookies, pudding mix, baking soda, and salt. In a small bowl, mash the peeled bananas with a fork (for bigger chunks of banana in your bread, mash less; for smaller chunks, mash more).

3   In a large bowl, combine the melted butter and brown sugar. Beat with a handheld mixer on medium speed or by hand with a whisk until smooth, about 2 minutes, or longer by hand. Add the eggs one at a time, beating to incorporate fully after each addition. Add the condensed milk and vanilla and beat until smooth, about 3 minutes. Switch to a spatula and gently fold in the mashed banana. Add the dry ingredients and fold just until no streaks of flour remain. Take care not to overmix!

4   Pour the batter into the prepared pan and use the spatula to smooth out the top. Bake for 65 to 80 minutes, until golden brown and cooked through; if you touch the top, it should spring back, and a toothpick inserted into the center of the bread should come out mostly clean. Check the bread halfway through; if the top is browning too quickly, loosely cover it with aluminum foil or reduce the oven temperature to 325°F.

5   Remove from the oven and let the bread cool completely in the pan, about 2 hours, before slicing and serving. Wrapped in foil or plastic, it will keep at room temperature for up to 2 days—and is even better the day after baking—or in the fridge for up to 1 week.

Cold eggs upset warm butter, but the great thing about banana bread is that it's very forgiving. If your batter *banana splits*, just keep mixing, just keep mixing, just keep mixing, mixing, mixing.

Blueberry Streusel Griddle Cakes

"Griddle cakes" is just a cute name for pancakes. The nutty salted streusel is cooked into the batter along with bursting blubes, making these call-'em-what-you-want cakes shine. Forget boring blueberry pancakes—we are in our Blueberry Streusel Griddle Cakes era, and I love that for us.

Makes 6 to 8 large pancakes

Streusel Topping

⅓ cup all-purpose flour

3 tablespoons salted butter, at room temperature (it should be very soft)

¼ cup rolled oats

2 tablespoons packed light brown sugar

¼ teaspoon ground cinnamon

⅓ cup finely chopped walnuts (optional)

Griddle Cakes

1½ cups all-purpose flour

½ cup rolled oats

2 tablespoons granulated sugar

2 teaspoons baking powder

½ teaspoon baking soda

¼ teaspoon kosher salt

1½ cups buttermilk, at room temperature

2 large eggs, at room temperature

2 tablespoons salted butter, melted and cooled

1 teaspoon pure vanilla extract

1 cup fresh blueberries, plus more for serving

Butter or nonstick cooking spray, for greasing

Maple syrup, for serving (optional)

Powdered sugar, for serving (optional)

The first pancake is always the hardest to flip, but don't quit. You'll do better next time . . . or at least by pancake number three.

1 **Make the streusel topping.** In a small bowl, stir together the flour and butter with a fork to make a thick paste. Add the oats, brown sugar, and cinnamon and mix until well combined; the mixture will be crumbly. Add the walnuts (if using) and toss to combine.

2 **Make the griddle cakes.** In a large bowl, whisk together the flour, oats, granulated sugar, baking powder, baking soda, and salt. In a separate large bowl, whisk together the buttermilk, eggs, melted butter, and vanilla until the mixture is well combined and smooth. Pour the wet ingredients into the dry ingredients and stir until just combined. Do not overmix—lumpy batter makes fluffy pancakes! Gently fold in the blueberries. Let the batter stand for 10 minutes.

3 Heat a griddle or large nonstick skillet over medium heat until hot. Lightly grease the surface with butter or cooking spray. Pour about ½ cup of the batter onto the griddle for each griddle cake, spreading it slightly into a circular shape and leaving at least 1 inch of space between each griddle cake. Sprinkle 1 heaping tablespoon of the streusel topping over each griddle cake. Cook, adjusting the heat as needed if the butter starts to smoke, until bubbles form on the surface of the griddle cakes and the edges look set, 2 to 3 minutes. Flip the griddle cakes and cook until golden brown on the other side and cooked through, 1 to 2 minutes more. Transfer the griddle cakes to a plate and repeat with the remaining batter and streusel topping (see Note), adding more butter or cooking spray to the griddle between batches if necessary.

4 To serve, top the griddle cakes with more blueberries and enjoy right away, with a drizzle of maple syrup and/or powdered sugar, if you like!

NOTE: Bake any leftover streusel at 350°F for 15 minutes, stirring after about 10 minutes, and use as garnish.

Chocolate Chip Scones

When I was a kid, Fridays were the special days we got to stop for a breakfast treat on the way to school. There wasn't a whole lot my sister and I agreed on at the time, but stopping at the little café down the street for a warm chocolate chip scone was one of them. Scones are a great car breakfast because they're pocket-size and handheld, kind of like a muffin that tastes like a cookie. Best of all, they're not too sweet—rather, they're just sweet enough. I feel like scones get a bad rap because most of the time they are full of polarizing things like raisins or citrus zest. I personally don't want either in my scone. I want chocolate chips, and I won't apologize for that.

Makes 8

2 cups all-purpose flour, plus more for dusting

¼ cup granulated sugar

1 teaspoon baking powder

½ teaspoon baking soda

¼ teaspoon kosher salt

½ cup (1 stick) unsalted butter, cut into small cubes and frozen for 20 to 30 minutes

1 cup semisweet chocolate chips (or whatever kind of chocolate your heart desires)

¾ cup plus 1 tablespoon buttermilk

1 teaspoon pure vanilla extract

1 tablespoon Demerara or turbinado sugar, for sprinkling (optional)

1   Preheat the oven to 400°F. Line a baking sheet with parchment paper.

2   In a large bowl, whisk together the flour, granulated sugar, baking powder, baking soda, and salt. Add the cold butter cubes and, using a pastry cutter or a fork, work the butter into the flour until the mixture looks like sand with some coarse pea-size crumbs. Fold in the chocolate chips.

3   In a small bowl, whisk together ¾ cup of the buttermilk and the vanilla. While stirring, slowly pour the wet mixture into the flour mixture and stir until just incorporated—be careful not to overmix. Gently work the dough with your hand just to bring it together and incorporate all the flour; again, do not overmix.

4   Turn the dough out onto a lightly floured work surface and gently shape it into a round, about 1½ inches thick. Cut the round into quarters, then cut each quarter in half again to create 8 wedges total. Transfer the wedges to the prepared baking sheet. Brush the tops with the remaining 1 tablespoon buttermilk and sprinkle with the Demerara sugar (if using).

5   Bake for 20 to 22 minutes, until the tops are golden brown and the scones are cooked through; if you poke them with a toothpick, it should come out clean. Transfer the scones to a wire rack to cool slightly, 10 to 20 minutes, then enjoy warm!

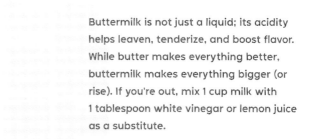

Buttermilk is not just a liquid; its acidity helps leaven, tenderize, and boost flavor. While butter makes everything better, buttermilk makes everything bigger (or rise). If you're out, mix 1 cup milk with 1 tablespoon white vinegar or lemon juice as a substitute.

Strawberry Short 'n' Sheet Cake

Is there anything not to like about strawberry shortcake? NO. Well, maybe the prep time. In an effort to make the world a better place, I managed to solve that problem. This sheet pan method simplifies the baking and cleanup so that the whole process is short 'n' sweet. This may be more of a giant biscuit than a cake, but who's complaining about that? I recommend saving this recipe for the summer because the strawberries are the star of this show. If you just can't wait, I don't blame you—use thawed frozen berries instead! Shortcake falls into the brunch category for me, but one girl's breakfast is another girl's dessert, so make it whenever you please, and don't sell yourself short, cake.

Serves 8 to 12

1½ pounds ripe strawberries, hulled and quartered

1 cup plus 1 tablespoon granulated sugar, plus more to taste

1 lemon, halved

Nonstick cooking spray

½ cup (1 stick) plus 1 tablespoon unsalted butter

4 cups all-purpose flour, plus more for dusting

5 teaspoons baking powder

2 teaspoons kosher salt

1½ cups buttermilk, plus more as needed

2½ cups heavy cream

1 tablespoon Demerara or turbinado sugar

1 teaspoon pure vanilla extract

1 cup sour cream or mascarpone cheese

1   Place half the strawberries in a medium bowl and gently crush with a fork to release their juices. Add the remaining strawberries and ¼ cup of the granulated sugar, then squeeze in some lemon juice and stir to combine. Taste the mixture; depending on your strawberries, it may need more sugar or lemon juice. Keep adjusting until it tastes good to you! Cover the bowl and set aside to macerate at room temperature for up to 2 hours.

2   Preheat the oven to 400°F. Line a 9×13-inch rimmed baking sheet with parchment paper, then coat the parchment with cooking spray.

3   Cut the ½ cup (1 stick) butter into small cubes and freeze them for 20 to 30 minutes. Melt the remaining 1 tablespoon butter in a small saucepan over medium heat, then let cool slightly.

4   In a large bowl, whisk together the flour, ¾ cup of the granulated sugar, the baking powder, and the salt. Remove the butter cubes from the freezer and use a pastry cutter or fork to mix them into the flour until the butter is broken down into pea-size pieces and evenly coated with flour. Add the buttermilk and ½ cup of the cream, and fold gently with a spatula until the dough just comes together. Knead the dough in the bowl very gently to incorporate any loose pieces of dough or flour; it will be sticky and a bit crumbly. If you can't incorporate all the flour into one ball, add more buttermilk 1 tablespoon at a time.

5   Dollop the dough onto the prepared baking sheet and, as lightly as you can, press it into an even layer from corner to corner. Don't compact the dough, but be sure there are no gaps in the pan—you're going for one giant biscuit here. Brush the dough with the melted butter and sprinkle with the Demerara sugar.

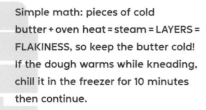

Simple math: pieces of cold butter + oven heat = steam = LAYERS = FLAKINESS, so keep the butter cold! If the dough warms while kneading, chill it in the freezer for 10 minutes then continue.

6 Bake for 25 to 30 minutes, until golden brown. Let the shortcake cool in the pan for 10 minutes, then carefully remove it from the pan and transfer it to a wire rack to cool completely, 1 to 2 hours.

7 Just before serving, in a large bowl, whip the remaining 2 cups cream with a handheld mixer on medium speed or by hand until soft peaks form (meaning when you stop mixing and lift out the beaters or whisk, the whipped cream forms a "mountain peak" but the top falls over), about 2 minutes, or longer by hand. Add the vanilla and remaining 1 tablespoon granulated sugar and beat until thick, stiff peaks form (now the peak stays standing!), 30 seconds more. Add the sour cream and gently fold with a spatula until just combined.

8 Transfer the cooled shortcake to a cutting board. Holding a serrated knife parallel to the cutting board, carefully cut the shortcake in half horizontally (it's delicate, so take your time, and steady it by putting your other hand on top of the cake while you slice). Carefully use a spatula or two to slide the top off and transfer it to a flat surface. Spread the bottom half of the shortcake with about half the whipped cream. Use a slotted spoon to lift about half the macerated strawberries from the bowl, leaving the juices behind (you can drizzle some on the assembled shortcake if you'd like), and place them on top of the whipped cream. Very carefully place the top half of the shortcake over the strawberries, then garnish with the remaining whipped cream and strawberries. Use the serrated knife to carefully cut the shortcake into individual servings. Enjoy!

Bananas Foster Cinnamon Rolls

Having just *one* banana-flavored recipe in this book didn't feel authentic to me as a person or a cook, so (contrary to my editor's advice) I managed to sneak another one in. Bananas Foster is a classic dessert that ignites the flavor of banana with delicious things like butter, brown sugar, cinnamon, and rum. And when I say "ignite," I mean it, because the dessert is literally set on fire. While we will not be lighting our cinnamon rolls on fire (well, not on purpose, anyway), they'll catch heat in the oven and turn into fluffy rolls of goodness. The closest I've come to heaven is taking a bite out of one of these cinnamon rolls. (Although they do feel pretty sinful, so maybe it's the closest I've ever come to hell.)

Makes 12

Dough and Filling

1 cup warm milk (about 110°F)

1 (¼-ounce) packet active dry yeast (2¼ teaspoons)

4 tablespoons (½ stick) plus ⅓ cup unsalted butter, plus more for greasing

½ cup granulated sugar

2 large eggs, at room temperature

4 cups bread flour, plus more for dusting

1 teaspoon kosher salt, plus more as needed

½ cup packed dark brown sugar

2 tablespoons dark rum

2 teaspoons ground cinnamon

½ teaspoon pure vanilla extract

2 small ripe bananas (they don't have to be *super* ripe here!), mashed

½ cup heavy cream, at room temperature

Cream Cheese Glaze

1 cup powdered sugar, plus more if needed

2 ounces cream cheese, at room temperature, plus more if needed

4 tablespoons (½ stick) unsalted butter, at room temperature (it should be very soft)

3 tablespoons heavy cream, plus more if needed

1 teaspoon pure vanilla extract

1 Make the dough. In a small bowl, combine the warm milk and yeast. Let stand until frothy, 5 to 10 minutes.

2 Meanwhile, melt ⅓ cup of the butter in a small saucepan over medium heat, then let cool slightly.

3 Grease a large bowl and a 9 × 13-inch baking dish with butter. In a separate large bowl, stir together the granulated sugar, melted butter, and eggs until smooth. Add the yeast mixture and stir well. While stirring, gradually add the flour and salt and stir until the dough comes together, then knead it by hand until soft, about 5 minutes. Place the dough in the greased bowl, cover with a damp kitchen towel and set aside to rise in a warm place until the dough is puffed up, 1 to 1½ hours; if you poke it with a finger, it should spring back but leave a slight indent.

4 Meanwhile, melt the remaining 4 tablespoons (½ stick) butter in the same saucepan over medium heat. Add the brown sugar, rum, cinnamon, vanilla, and a pinch of salt. Stir to combine, then cook, without stirring, until the mixture is syrupy and beginning to bubble, about 2 minutes; be careful not to let it burn! Add the bananas and stir to combine. Reduce the heat to medium-low and cook, stirring occasionally, until warmed through and well combined, 3 to 4 minutes more. Pour the filling into a medium bowl and set aside to cool and thicken.

5 To assemble the rolls, punch down the dough and turn it out onto a lightly floured surface. Roll out the dough to a roughly 12 × 16-inch rectangle (I usually just eyeball this, but try to make the sides straight and the shape even so it rolls nicely!), sprinkling it with flour as needed so it doesn't stick. Position the rectangle of dough with one long side closest to you. Spread the filling over the dough in an even layer, leaving about 1 inch of dough exposed around the edges.

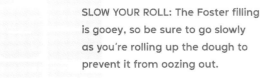

SLOW YOUR ROLL: The Foster filling is gooey, so be sure to go slowly as you're rolling up the dough to prevent it from oozing out.

6 Starting with the edge closest to you, slowly and carefully lift and roll the dough up and away from you to enclose the filling and prevent spillage, keeping the shape as smooth and even as you can, until the entire rectangle is rolled up into a log. Gently turn it seam-side down and use a serrated knife to trim the uneven ends, then cut the log crosswise into twelve even rolls. Place the rolls cut-side down in the prepared baking dish, spacing them evenly. Cover the dish with a kitchen towel and set aside in a warm place to rise until the rolls are puffed and touching, about 1 hour.

7 Preheat the oven to 350°F.

8 Pour the heavy cream evenly over the rolls (this will help keep them gooey and moist). Bake for 25 to 30 minutes, until golden brown.

9 **Meanwhile, make the glaze.** In a medium bowl, combine the powdered sugar, cream cheese, butter, heavy cream, and vanilla and beat with a handheld mixer on medium speed or a spatula until the glaze is smooth and pourable. If it's too thick, add a splash more cream; if it's too thin, add more cream cheese or powdered sugar.

10 Remove the cinnamon rolls from the oven and let cool until warm, about 15 minutes. Drizzle the glaze over the warm rolls and serve immediately.

Billionaire's Bacon

When I was growing up in the suburbs of San Francisco, a little restaurant in the city shot to popularity simply because of their delicious bacon (a good lesson that sometimes one brilliant idea is all it takes). The bacon was both sweet and spicy—not to mention its perfect balance of chewiness to crispiness. They called it Billonaire's Bacon. A lot has changed since I was a kid, including prices, so I'm calling my version Billion-Dollar Bacon, you know, to account for inflation. I thought this title was really original but apparently Snoop Dogg beat me to it. It's okay, though—as someone who was born on 4/20 and also loves Martha Stewart, it just means Snoop and I have one more thing in common. No, I am not a billionaire, but I do have stacks . . . of bacon.

1   Preheat the oven to 350°F. Line a baking sheet with aluminum foil and set a wire rack on top, if you've got one.

2   Arrange the bacon slices on the rack (or directly on the foil) in a single layer.

3   In a small bowl, mix together the brown sugar, red pepper flakes, and cinnamon until well combined. Sprinkle half the brown sugar mixture over the bacon, pressing it in to help it stick.

4   Bake for 15 minutes, then remove the pan from the oven and carefully flip each piece of bacon. Sprinkle evenly with the remaining brown sugar mixture and bake for 15 to 20 minutes more, until the bacon is brown and crispy on the edges and delightfully chewy in the middle.

Serves 4

8 slices thick-cut bacon

½ cup packed light brown sugar

1 tablespoon red pepper flakes

1 teaspoon ground cinnamon

HOT TIP

Billionaires have stacks, but for this bacon, we need racks. The rack allows the fat to drip away, resulting in crispy goodness.

Cheddar & Herb Skillet Hash Brown

In my humble opinion, McDonald's has perfected the hash brown. It's greasy, salty, and pocket-size—what's not to love? Naturally, when I create recipes, I pull ideas from my own taste and references, and hash browns are up there among my favorite breakfast foods. I usually only eat McDonald's hash browns the morning after a big night out, and I won't tell you to stop that post-party ritual—especially because this recipe takes some work and, if you're anything like me, is not one to make while hungover. What I *will* say is that it's a supersize take on a hash brown that delivers on flavor and fun, filled with herbs and cheese and oily happiness. Maybe I should have called it a Happy Brown.

Serves 4 to 6

3 pounds russet potatoes (about 3 large), peeled

½ cup fresh parsley, finely chopped, plus more for serving

¼ cup fresh dill, finely chopped, plus more for serving

1½ teaspoons kosher salt

Freshly ground black pepper

½ cup vegetable oil

1 cup freshly grated cheddar cheese

¼ cup sliced scallion

Flaky salt, for serving

All water and a light squeeze makes this hash a soggy potato. When I tell you to squeeze the water out of the potatoes, I mean it.

1   Shred the potatoes on the largest holes of a box grater. Rinse the shredded potatoes under cool water in a colander until the water runs clear. Place them on a kitchen towel and twist the ends to enclose the potatoes. Holding the towel over the sink, twist and squeeze firmly to drain off as much liquid as you can. Transfer the potatoes to a large bowl and add the parsley, dill, salt, and as much pepper as you like. Toss to mix evenly.

2   Heat ¼ cup of the oil in a large nonstick skillet over medium-high heat. When the oil is shimmering, add half the potato mixture and use a spatula to press it into an even layer over the bottom of the pan. Sprinkle evenly with the cheese and scallion, top with the remaining potato mixture, and press again to smooth out the top. Cook, rotating the pan occasionally, until golden and crispy on the bottom, about 15 minutes.

3   Now we have to flip this thing—remember, confidence is key! Carefully pour off any oil remaining in the skillet into a small heatproof bowl, holding the hash brown in the skillet with the spatula as you do. Carefully slide the hash brown onto a plate that's bigger than the skillet, then flip the skillet upside down and place it over the plate. Hold it steady while protecting your hands with a kitchen towel! Quickly flip the skillet and plate over together so the hash brown is back in the skillet with the browned side facing up. Return the pan to medium-high heat and cook for about 2 minutes to set the potatoes, then carefully lift up an edge and pour the remaining ¼ cup oil underneath the hash brown. Cook, rotating the pan occasionally, until the bottom is as golden brown and crispy as the top, 15 minutes more. Remove from the heat.

4   You can serve the hash brown straight from the skillet or slide it onto a plate and cut it into wedges. Sprinkle with flaky salt and more herbs and enjoy!

Smoky, Spicy Chipotle Shakshuka

When I was an intern at Tasty and applying to move up into a producer role, I was asked to make a recipe live in front of some very important people. I chose shakshuka because while it's an impressive and delicious dish, it's really quite simple to cook—and therefore good for tricking people into thinking you put in a lot of time in the kitchen. Apparently, it's also a good dish to trick people into giving you a job. This shakshuka packs quite the flavor punch and has the perfect balance of smokiness and spiciness to wake you up in the morning.

Serves 3 or 4

1 (28-ounce) can whole peeled tomatoes, with their juices

2 canned chipotle peppers in adobo, or 2 tablespoons pureed chipotle in adobo

1 tablespoon extra-virgin olive oil

1 medium onion, diced

1 red bell pepper, diced

2 garlic cloves, minced or grated

1 teaspoon ground cumin

1 teaspoon smoked paprika

½ teaspoon chipotle chile powder

1 tablespoon tomato paste

1 to 3 teaspoons harissa, to taste

Kosher salt and freshly ground black pepper

6 or 8 large eggs

For Serving

Crumbled feta cheese

Fresh dill

Yogurt, labneh, or sour cream

1   In a blender or food processor, combine the whole tomatoes and their juices with the chipotles and blend on medium-high speed until smooth, about 1 minute.

2   Heat the olive oil in a large skillet over medium heat. When the oil is shimmering, add the onion and cook, stirring often, until soft and translucent, about 7 minutes. Add the bell pepper and garlic and cook, stirring frequently, until the pepper begins to soften, 3 minutes or so. Stir in the cumin, paprika, and chipotle powder and cook, stirring, until fragrant, about 1 minute. Add the tomato paste and harissa and cook, stirring continuously, until fragrant, about 2 minutes, adjusting the heat as needed if the mixture starts to scorch.

3   Pour the blended chipotle-tomato mixture into the pan and stir well to combine fully. Reduce the heat to low and simmer, stirring occasionally, until the flavors meld and the sauce has reduced slightly, about 15 minutes. Taste and season with salt and black pepper to your liking.

4   Make six or eight small wells in the sauce with a spoon (one for each egg) and crack an egg into each well. Season the eggs with salt and black pepper. Cover the skillet and cook until the egg whites are set and the yolks are cooked to your desired level of doneness, 5 to 8 minutes for runny yolks, a few minutes longer for firmer yolks. Remove from the heat.

5   Sprinkle the shakshuka with feta and dill and bring the pan to the table. Enjoy immediately, with some yogurt spooned over each serving to help temper the spice!

If you're spice-shy, skip the harissa—chipotles bring enough heat on their own! But if you're feeling bold, add the harissa slowly, tasting as you go.

Three-Cheese Dutch Baby
WITH CHIVE BACON BUTTER

When I was a little girl, I used to think everything that had something to do with my life meant it belonged to me. For instance, I genuinely believed the Dutch baby, a crispy pancake inflated like a popover, was my family's invention because of its name and our Dutch heritage. I now know the truth—that the Dutch baby isn't even Dutch, let alone a family heirloom—but that doesn't make it any less delicious. I may not have invented it, but I'm proud to claim my savory take on this showstopping dish as my own.

Serves 4

3 large eggs, at room temperature

½ cup all-purpose flour

½ cup whole milk, at room temperature

½ teaspoon kosher salt

¼ teaspoon freshly ground black pepper

6 slices bacon

2 tablespoons freshly grated Gruyère cheese

2 tablespoons freshly grated sharp cheddar cheese

4 tablespoons (½ stick) unsalted butter, at room temperature

2 tablespoons finely chopped fresh chives, plus more for serving

2 tablespoons freshly grated Parmigiano Reggiano cheese, for serving

While your Dutch baby is baking, DON'T PEEK. The sudden temperature drop from opening the oven can lead to a flat baby, making you cry like one.

1   In a blender or food processor, combine the eggs, flour, milk, salt, and pepper. Blend on low speed until smooth, about 30 seconds. The batter should be runny. Let stand at room temperature for 30 minutes to allow the flour to fully absorb the liquid and hydrate.

2   Meanwhile, position a rack in the center of the oven and remove any racks above it. Lay the bacon slices in a single layer in a 9- to 10-inch cast-iron or other oven-safe skillet and place it on the oven rack. Preheat the oven to 425°F.

3   Check on the bacon after 10 to 15 minutes—it should be crisp and the fat should be rendered. If the top isn't browning as fast as the bottom, flip the slices and bake for a few minutes more. Remove the pan from the oven and transfer the bacon to a cutting board to cool (keep the oven on). Carefully swirl the hot pan to coat the bottom and sides with the rendered bacon fat.

4   Add the Gruyère and cheddar to the batter and stir to combine evenly, then pour the batter into the hot skillet and return it to the oven. Bake the Dutch baby for 12 to 20 minutes, until golden and puffed. The sides will be darker in color than the middle.

5   Meanwhile, crumble 2 slices of the bacon into a small bowl (reserve the rest for serving). Add the butter and chives and mix until well combined. Refrigerate the butter while the Dutch baby bakes.

6   Remove the Dutch baby from the oven and place it on something heatproof on your table. Serve it straight from the pan, with a dollop of the chive butter in the center and the Parm sprinkled over everything. Cut the Dutch baby into wedges and enjoy while it's hot, with even more chive butter and the remaining bacon on the side.

Green Eggs & Ham Sandwich

I like to think of myself as a big kid, or better yet, an adult with a little-kid spirit. No recipe screams "childhood" more than green eggs and ham, but much like I have grown up, this recipe has, too. I can't say I enjoyed spinach much as a kid, so this is an elevated take on a nostalgic dish that caters perfectly to a well-developed palate, a playful heart, and a craving for a great breakfast sandy. In the wise words of Dr. Seuss's Sam-I-Am:

You do not like them. So you say.
Try them! Try them! And you may.

Serves 4

1 cup packed baby spinach

¼ cup fresh basil leaves

¼ cup fresh parsley

2 tablespoons freshly grated Parmigiano Reggiano cheese

¼ cup extra-virgin olive oil, plus more as needed

Kosher salt and freshly ground black pepper

4 slices Canadian bacon or cooked ham

2 tablespoons unsalted butter

4 brioche buns

4 large eggs

2 tablespoons mayonnaise or labneh

Sliced avocado, for serving (optional)

Hot sauce, for serving (optional)

HOT TIP

When frying eggs, stick with a nonstick pan.

1   In a blender or food processor, combine the spinach, basil, parsley, Parm, and olive oil and season with salt and pepper. Blend on medium-high speed until you have a smooth green paste, 2 minutes, adding more olive oil 1 tablespoon at a time as needed if the paste is very thick. Taste and season with more salt and pepper to your liking.

2   Heat a large nonstick skillet over medium heat. When the pan is hot, place the ham slices in the pan and cook until just warmed through, 1 to 2 minutes on each side. Transfer the ham to a plate.

3   In the same skillet, melt 1 tablespoon of the butter over medium heat. Place half the buns in the pan, cut-side down, and toast until golden and crisp, 3 to 4 minutes. Transfer to a large plate or cutting board. Repeat with the remaining 1 tablespoon butter and remaining buns.

4   Crack the eggs into the pan, leaving some room between them, and season with salt and pepper. Pour some of the green sauce on top of each egg (the oil in the sauce will help fry the eggs), reserving about 2 tablespoons for the sandwiches. Cover and cook until the egg whites are set but the yolks are still slightly runny, 2 to 3 minutes.

5   In a small bowl, mix the reserved green sauce with the mayonnaise. Assemble the breakfast sandwiches by slathering the green sauce mixture on the bottom buns. Place a slice of ham on each bottom bun and carefully place one green egg on top. Add sliced avocado and/or hot sauce, if you like. Finish the sandwiches with the bun tops and enjoy immediately!

Peaches & Sour Cream Pound Cake

My friend had a recipe for sour cream pound cake that we would make for breakfast every time we had a sleepover in elementary school. We would look forward to the weekends not because we didn't have to go to school, but because we knew it was time to make that pound cake. It's a bit of a sophisticated thing for kids to love, but once you taste it, you'll know exactly why we did—the tanginess of the sour cream perfectly balances out the richness of the cake. The recipe I made as a kid is great, but in adulthood, it hit me like a stone (fruit): *ADD PEACHES!* Their sweet succulence results in a pound cake that's as charmingly moist as it is irresistible. Each bite bursts with the juiciness of ripe peaches, while the sour cream ensures a decadently tender crumb. It's peach perfect!

Serves 6 to 8

1 cup (2 sticks) unsalted butter, at room temperature, plus more for greasing

2½ cups all-purpose flour, plus more for dusting

2 or 3 ripe peaches, peeled, pitted, and diced, or 10 ounces frozen diced peaches, thawed

2 cups plus 2 tablespoons granulated sugar, plus more to taste

½ lemon

4 large eggs, at room temperature

1½ cups sour cream, at room temperature

1 teaspoon pure vanilla extract

½ teaspoon baking powder

¼ teaspoon kosher salt

1 cup heavy cream

Powdered sugar, for dusting

1   Preheat the oven to 325°F. Grease a 10-inch Bundt pan with butter, then dust the inside with flour to coat and tap out any excess. Be sure the pan is well coated to prevent sticking.

2   In a small bowl, combine the peaches, 1 tablespoon of the granulated sugar, and a small squeeze of lemon juice. Toss gently to coat the peaches. Taste and add more lemon juice or sugar as needed—it should be pleasantly sweet and tart. Set aside to let the flavors meld while you prepare the batter.

3   In a large bowl, combine the butter and 2 cups of the granulated sugar. Using a handheld mixer, beat on medium speed until light and fluffy, about 2 minutes. Add the eggs one at a time, beating to incorporate fully after each addition and stopping to scrape down the sides of the bowl as needed. Add 1 cup of the sour cream and the vanilla and beat on medium speed until just combined, about 1 minute.

4   In a medium bowl, whisk together the flour, baking powder, and salt. Gradually add the dry ingredients to the wet, using a spatula to mix until just combined. The batter will be very thick. Use a slotted spoon to lift the peaches from their bowl, leaving behind any liquid, and add them to the batter. Gently fold to distribute them evenly. Pour the batter into the prepared pan, spreading it evenly and smoothing out the top with the spatula.

5   Bake for 60 to 70 minutes, until a toothpick inserted into the center of the cake comes out clean. Remove from the oven and let cool in the pan for 15 minutes (see Hot Tip, page 50), then carefully invert the cake onto a wire rack and let cool completely, 1 to 2 hours.

I'm here to remind you to cool your Bundts off. No, but literally, cool them off before you attempt to flip the cake. Timing is everything: If you flip it too soon, it may fall apart; if you let it cool too long, it may stick.

6   Meanwhile, in a large bowl, whip the cream with a handheld mixer on medium speed or by hand until soft peaks form (meaning when you stop mixing and lift out the beaters or whisk, the whipped cream forms a "mountain peak" but the top falls over), about 2 minutes, or longer by hand. Add the remaining ½ cup sour cream and remaining 1 tablespoon granulated sugar and beat until thick, stiff peaks form (now the peak stays standing!), 30 seconds more.

7   When the cake has completely cooled, dust it with powdered sugar (see Hot Tip, page 253) for a touch of extra sweetness. Slice and enjoy with the whipped cream alongside.

Caramelized Onion & Blistered Tomato Breakfast Galette

I love a good fancy word for a simple thing, and from "chiffonade" to "mise en place," the cooking vocabulary happens to have a lot of them. But sometimes fancy words (or is it just French words?) have the power to intimidate. Maybe "galette" provokes an urge within you to turn to the next page. To that I say HOLD ON—don't swipe left just yet. If you knew "galette" was just another word for a flat round crust that's partially folded over a filling and baked right on a baking sheet, no pie dish necessary, would it all sound a little more inviting? Galettes are rustic and forgiving. I also happen to love the word "rustic" because it's a fancy term for something simple, homey, and imperfect. Rustic as this galette is, the richness of the caramelized onions and the juiciness of the blistered tomatoes will have you feeling fancy AF.

Serves 4 to 6

½ cup (1 stick) plus 1 tablespoon unsalted butter

1¼ cups all-purpose flour, plus more for dusting

2 tablespoons finely chopped fresh dill, plus more for serving

½ teaspoon kosher salt, plus more as needed

3 to 4 tablespoons ice water, as needed

2 tablespoons extra-virgin olive oil

1 large yellow onion, thinly sliced

½ teaspoon ground turmeric

¼ teaspoon red pepper flakes

1 tablespoon tomato paste

2 cups cherry tomatoes

2 garlic cloves, minced or grated

Freshly ground black pepper

3 large eggs

Freshly grated Parmigiano Reggiano cheese, for serving

Labneh, for serving

1   Cut ½ cup (1 stick) of the butter into small cubes and freeze them for 20 to 30 minutes.

2   In a large bowl, combine the flour, dill, and salt. Remove the butter cubes from the freezer and use a pastry cutter or a fork to cut them into the flour until you get coarse crumbs with pea-size pieces of butter. Gradually add the ice water, 1 tablespoon at a time, and mix until all the flour is incorporated and the dough comes together. Form the dough into a ball, flatten it into a disc, wrap it in plastic wrap, and refrigerate to let the dough relax, at least 30 minutes or up to overnight.

3   In a large skillet, heat 1 tablespoon of the olive oil with the remaining 1 tablespoon butter over medium heat. When the butter has melted, add the onion and stir to coat. Cook, stirring often, until the onion is soft and beginning to color, about 10 minutes. Season with a generous pinch of salt. Reduce the heat to medium-low and cook, stirring occasionally, until the onion is brown and caramelized, 30 minutes more. Add 1 tablespoon water to hydrate the caramelized onions for a more jamlike texture.

4   Add the turmeric and red pepper flakes and stir to coat the onions. Add the tomato paste, stir to combine, and cook for about 3 minutes to develop the flavor of the paste. Increase the heat to medium and add the remaining 1 tablespoon olive oil and the cherry tomatoes. Cook, stirring occasionally and scraping the bottom of the pan to avoid burning, until the tomatoes are blistered and lightly browned, 7 to 10 minutes. Add the garlic and cook for 1 minute more, just until fragrant. Remove the skillet from the heat and season with salt and black pepper to your liking. Toss gently to combine.

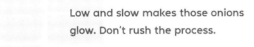

Low and slow makes those onions glow. Don't rush the process.

5 Preheat the oven to 400°F. Line a baking sheet with parchment paper.

6 Lightly flour a work surface. Unwrap the chilled dough and use a rolling pin (or a wine bottle, I won't judge) to roll it out into a 12-inch round. To get an even disc, roll in one direction, rotating the dough a quarter turn after each roll and sprinkling with more flour as needed to prevent the dough from sticking. Transfer the dough to the prepared baking sheet. Arrange the caramelized onion mixture in the center of the dough, leaving 2 inches exposed around the edge. Create 3 wells in the onion mixture with a spoon (these will hold the eggs, but don't add them yet). Fold the dough from the edge over the filling, leaving the center exposed and overlapping the folds to create a rustic round shape; if the dough begins to warm up too much, stick the galette into the freezer for 10 minutes to firm it up before continuing.

7 Bake for about 30 minutes, until the crust is cooked through and golden brown, then remove from the oven and crack one egg into each well in the onions. Sprinkle the eggs with salt and black pepper. Bake for about 10 minutes more, until the egg whites are almost set (they'll finish cooking as the galette rests). Remove from the oven and let cool slightly, about 10 minutes.

8 Garnish with dill and freshly grated Parm. Slice the galette, cutting through each egg yolk so every serving gets a bit of egg, and serve immediately, with labneh!

2

SALADS,

SOUPS,

AND

SANDYS

Green Goblin Salad
(GREEN GODDESS'S SPICY COUSIN)

I'm sure you all know of Green Goddess by now: She's pristine and clean. Listen, I like her, but she's had her moment, and you are not here for the clean girl aesthetic. I think it's about time we all unleash our inner goblins and embrace our hot mess. The Green Goblin is as delicious as the Goddess, but the Goblin is for those moments when you're feeling frisky and debaucherous. We are turning up more than just the heat, and this salad will be your new partner in crime.

SERVES 4 TO 6 AS A SIDE, OR 2 OR 3 AS A MAIN

Spicy Green Goblin Dressing

½ cup plain full-fat Greek yogurt

½ cup fresh parsley

½ cup mixed fresh herbs, such as mint, basil, dill, and/or tarragon

¼ cup fresh cilantro

1 tablespoon chopped fresh chives

2 tablespoons pine nuts, toasted

1 tablespoon seasoned rice vinegar

½ jalapeño, some seeds removed (or not, for spice!), chopped

½ small shallot, chopped

1 small garlic clove, peeled

1 teaspoon drained capers

1 lemon, halved

Kosher salt and freshly ground black pepper

Salad

1 large head leafy lettuce (I like butter lettuce), leaves separated and chopped or torn, or 6 cups thinly sliced green cabbage

2 Persian cucumbers, diced

1 avocado, diced

¼ cup pine nuts, toasted, for serving

1 Make the dressing. In a blender or food processor, combine the yogurt, all the herbs, the pine nuts, vinegar, jalapeño, shallot, garlic, and capers. Squeeze a little juice from one lemon half into the blender and season with salt and pepper. Pulse the machine in very short bursts, scraping down the sides as needed, until well combined and creamy; how many pulses will depend on your machine, but it may seem like it's never going to happen and then all of the sudden—bam!—you've got dressing, so be patient. Taste and season with more lemon juice, salt, and/or pepper to your liking.

2 Make the salad. In a large bowl, combine the lettuce, cucumbers, and avocado. Drizzle with the dressing to taste and toss to combine. Sprinkle with the pine nuts before serving.

Never get dressed too early. (I'm talking about the salad.)

Warm Brussels Sprout & Leek Salad

WITH HONEY DIJON DRESSING

Salad season may be in the summer, but let me introduce you to one that defies the seasons—an evergreen salad, if you will. This recipe shatters all the salad stereotypes we've been fed, trading in cool and crisp for warm and cozy, and proving that NO ONE PUTS SALAD IN A CORNER. With tender Brussels sprouts and leeks roasted to perfection and a honey Dijon dressing drizzling like a fall rain, this salad will be your companion from fall into winter into spring and right through into summer.

SERVES 4 TO 6 AS A SIDE, OR 2 OR 3 AS A MAIN

Leeks and Brussels Sprouts

2 medium leeks, white and light green parts only, thinly sliced and cleaned (see Hot Tip, page 236)

1½ pounds Brussels sprouts, trimmed and thinly sliced or shaved

2 tablespoons extra-virgin olive oil

Kosher salt and freshly ground black pepper

Dressing

¼ cup extra-virgin olive oil

2 tablespoons apple cider vinegar

1 tablespoon Dijon mustard

1 tablespoon honey

Kosher salt and freshly ground black pepper

Salad

¼ cup pine nuts, toasted

¼ cup dried currants or cranberries

½ cup crumbled feta cheese

1 Preheat the oven to 400°F. Line two baking sheets with parchment paper.

2 Make the leeks and Brussels sprouts. Spread the leeks and Brussels sprouts over the prepared baking sheets and drizzle with the olive oil. Season with salt and pepper and toss to coat. Roast for 30 to 35 minutes, stirring and rotating the pans after 20 minutes, until tender and lightly browned.

3 Meanwhile, make the dressing. In a small bowl, whisk together the olive oil, vinegar, mustard, and honey and season with salt and pepper. Taste and adjust the seasoning to your liking.

4 In a large bowl, combine the roasted Brussels sprouts and leeks, pine nuts, and currants. Drizzle the dressing over the salad to taste and toss to coat evenly. Top with the feta and serve immediately.

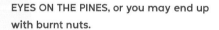

EYES ON THE PINES, or you may end up with burnt nuts.

Apple & Toasted Walnut Salad
WITH CREAMY LABNEH DRESSING

Some salads are all bark and no bite. This one is both. If you, too, have been wilted by sad and soggy salads in the past, let me introduce you to one that's crunchy, crisp, tangy, and irresistibly creamy. This is not a regular salad—it's a cool salad, both literally and figuratively. I love salad with fruit in it because it offers a cooling, refreshing, and juicy twist (that's the bark). Along with the sturdy cabbage, the walnuts and apples offer some serious crunch (that's the bite). That's what I like most out of a salad—I want some resistance when I chew, you know? This salad will make you work for it, and while it may resist you, you won't be able to resist it.

SERVES 4 TO 6 AS A SIDE, OR 2 OR 3 AS A MAIN

Dressing

½ cup labneh or plain full-fat Greek yogurt

¼ cup fresh dill, finely chopped

2 tablespoons extra-virgin olive oil

1 tablespoon honey

1 garlic clove, minced or grated

Kosher salt and freshly ground black pepper

Juice of ½ lemon, plus more as needed

Salad

1 small head green cabbage, thinly sliced

1 cup walnuts, toasted and chopped

½ small red onion, shaved or very thinly sliced

1 green apple, cored and thinly sliced (see Hot Tip)

Flaky salt, for serving

1 Make the dressing. In a small bowl, whisk together the labneh, dill, olive oil, honey, and garlic and season with salt and pepper. Whisk in the lemon juice. Taste and season with more salt, pepper, and/or lemon juice to your liking.

2 Make the salad. In a large serving bowl, combine the cabbage, walnuts, onion, and apple. Spoon the dressing over the salad to taste and toss to coat evenly. Sprinkle with flaky salt and serve immediately, or hold off on the salt and chill in the fridge for up to 1 hour, then sprinkle with salt and serve.

HOT TIP

How do you like them apples? Not brown. After you slice your apples, immediately toss them in lemon juice to keep them from oxidizing.

Garlicky Grilled Caesar Salad
WITH BROWN BUTTER BREADCRUMBS

The Caesar salad: one of food's greatest icons. How has it managed to stay relevant after all these years? Maybe Caesar is up there pulling some strings. My modern take on the classic is garlicky, grilled to perfection, and sprinkled with nutty brown butter breadcrumbs—is a reminder that continued evolution is a key ingredient to a long and flavorful life. So embrace the power of change in your own life, because legends that evolve never die.

SERVES 6 AS A SIDE, OR 3 AS A MAIN

Dressing

¼ cup freshly grated Parmigiano Reggiano cheese, plus more for serving

3 garlic cloves, minced or grated

2 oil-packed anchovy fillets, finely chopped or mashed, or 1 tablespoon drained capers, finely chopped

2 large egg yolks

1 tablespoon Dijon mustard

½ teaspoon Worcestershire sauce

Juice of ½ lemon, plus more as needed

1 cup extra-virgin olive oil

Kosher salt and freshly ground black pepper

Salad

2 tablespoons unsalted butter

1 cup panko or plain breadcrumbs

Kosher salt

3 large heads romaine lettuce, stem ends trimmed (but left on!) and heads halved lengthwise

Torn fresh dill, for serving

1   Heat the grill to medium-high. (If you don't have a grill, you can use a grill pan or a large cast-iron skillet, but hold off on heating it for now.)

2   **Make the dressing.** In a large bowl, whisk together the Parm, garlic, anchovies, egg yolks, mustard, Worcestershire, and lemon juice until well combined. While whisking continuously, very slowly drizzle in the olive oil—add it just a drop at a time until it forms a creamy emulsion, then you can start adding it a little faster—then whisk until the dressing thickens and becomes creamy. Taste and season with salt, pepper, and more lemon juice to your liking. If the dressing is very thick, whisk in water a splash at a time until it's thick and creamy but drizzle-able. Refrigerate until ready to serve.

3   **Make the salad.** Melt the butter in a small saucepan or skillet over medium heat, then cook, stirring continuously with a spatula, until it turns golden brown and has a nutty aroma, about 2 minutes. Be careful not to burn it! Add the breadcrumbs and toss to coat evenly. Cook, stirring often, until the breadcrumbs are golden brown—be careful not to burn them, either!—2 to 3 minutes. Remove from the heat, season with salt, and transfer to a plate to cool.

4   If you're using the stovetop, now's the time to heat your grill pan or cast-iron skillet over high heat until very hot.

5   Place the romaine cut-side down on the hot grill or pan (work in batches if using a pan). Grill until the romaine is slightly charred on the bottom but not completely heated through or overly wilted, about 4 minutes.

6   Transfer the grilled romaine to a serving plate, cut-side up, and drizzle with the dressing to taste. Sprinkle with the brown butter breadcrumbs, more Parm, and some dill. Serve immediately!

No one likes limp leaves. Use a hot preheated grill or grill pan for a quick, swift sear to achieve the char but preserve the crunch.

Crispy Rice Salad

What does it say about me that my two favorite kinds of salad are bread salad and rice salad—both of which made it into this cookbook? Just like a horoscope, I believe our food choices say a lot about us. As a Taurus, I'm all about indulgence, which probably explains the added carbs. This crispy rice salad, in particular, is packed with herbs and a savory soy dressing. If you've got leftover rice and a bunch of herbs in your fridge, this is your next meal . . . No leftover rice? No worries—just cook some, spread it over a baking sheet in an even layer, and let it cool completely in the fridge before frying for the crispiest crunch.

SERVES 4 AS A SIDE, OR 2 AS A MAIN

Dressing

¼ cup low-sodium soy sauce

¼ cup rice vinegar

2 tablespoons honey

1 tablespoon toasted sesame oil

1 tablespoon grated fresh ginger

2 garlic cloves, minced or grated

Freshly ground black pepper

Salad

¼ cup vegetable oil

2 cups leftover long-grain white rice

Kosher salt

4 cups finely chopped lettuce leaves of your choice (I use Little Gems)

1 cup fresh cilantro, coarsely chopped

½ cup fresh mint leaves, coarsely chopped

½ cup fresh basil leaves, coarsely chopped

2 Persian cucumbers, finely chopped

2 scallions, thinly sliced

½ red bell pepper (or a whole one, if you love it!), finely chopped

For Serving

1 small jalapeño, thinly sliced (seeded if you want less heat)

¼ cup chopped roasted peanuts

Sesame seeds

Lime wedges

1 Make the dressing. In a small bowl, whisk together the soy sauce, vinegar, honey, sesame oil, ginger, and garlic until well combined. Season with black pepper.

2 Make the salad. Heat the vegetable oil in a medium skillet over high heat. Line a plate with paper towels. When the oil is shimmering, add the rice and cook, stirring just a few times to break up any large clumps, until crispy and golden brown, 6 to 7 minutes (or possibly longer, depending on how moist the rice is). Use a slotted spoon to transfer the crispy rice to the paper towels to drain and sprinkle with salt.

3 In a large bowl, combine the lettuce, cilantro, mint, basil, cucumbers, scallions, bell pepper, and crispy fried rice. Drizzle with the dressing to taste and toss well to combine.

4 Top the salad with the jalapeño and sprinkle with the peanuts and sesame seeds. Serve with lime wedges on the side.

To get a good tan, you lay out in the sun for a long time and only flip over when you're ready. Same goes here. Let the rice fry in the oil without moving it to let the bottom layer develop a crispy crust and golden glow.

Coconut-Ginger Pumpkin Soup
WITH CRISPY FRIED SAGE & GARLIC CHIPS

I am a soup girlie. I love that it's hot, I love that you eat it with a spoon, I love that it's easy to cook . . . I love it when it's smooth, when it's chunky, when it's creamy or funky. And while we're on the topic of love, this particular soup holds a special place in my heart because I made it when Zoya and I began *seriously* dating. There is fun, innocent, no-strings-attached dating and then there is the oh-shit-this-could-be-the-real-deal dating (spoiler alert: it is). Zoya and I took a few months to cross from the former to the latter, and maybe this soup was a good little push. A serious soup, if you will, and definitely the real deal. As I stirred the pot, the fragrant aromas of coconut, ginger, and pumpkin filled the air like pheromones, and if that weren't enough, the crispy sage and garlic chips on top sealed the deal.

SERVES 4

Soup

1 sugar pie pumpkin or medium butternut squash, quartered and seeded (see Note)

2 tablespoons extra-virgin olive oil, plus more as needed

1 medium yellow onion, diced

3 garlic cloves, minced or grated

1 green apple, cored and chopped

1 (1-inch) piece fresh ginger, peeled and grated

4 cups low-sodium vegetable stock

½ cup full-fat coconut milk

Kosher salt and freshly ground black pepper

For the Toppings

¼ cup extra-virgin olive oil, plus more as needed

4 garlic cloves, sliced

Kosher salt

7 to 10 fresh sage leaves

1 sourdough baguette, sliced

Red pepper flakes

1 **Make the soup.** Preheat the oven to 425°F.

2 Rub the pumpkin all over with olive oil and place cut-side down on a baking sheet. Roast until soft and easily pierced with a fork, about 30 minutes. Remove from the oven and let cool on the baking sheet for 5 minutes. Carefully peel the pumpkin (the skin should come off easily!); discard the skin and transfer the pumpkin flesh to a bowl.

3 Heat the olive oil in a large pot or Dutch oven over medium heat. When the oil is shimmering, add the onion and cook, stirring occasionally, until soft and translucent, about 7 minutes. Add the garlic and cook, stirring often, until fragrant, another minute.

4 Add the pumpkin, apple, and ginger to the pot, then add the stock and coconut milk. Season with salt and pepper. Bring to a simmer, then reduce the heat to medium-low and cook until the apple is soft and the flavors have combined, 5 to 7 minutes.

5 Use an immersion blender to blend the soup directly in the pot until smooth (see Hot Tip, page 68). Taste again and season with salt and pepper to your liking. Keep warm over low heat.

6 **Make the toppings**. Line a plate with paper towels. Heat the olive oil in a small skillet over medium heat. When the oil is shimmering, add the garlic and cook, stirring often, until lightly golden and crispy, about 5 minutes. Use a slotted spoon to transfer the garlic to the paper towels to drain, reserving the oil in the pan. Season the garlic with salt.

7 Add the sage to the hot oil and cook until crispy—this takes just a minute! Use a slotted spoon to transfer the

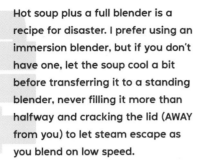

Hot soup plus a full blender is a recipe for disaster. I prefer using an immersion blender, but if you don't have one, let the soup cool a bit before transferring it to a standing blender, never filling it more than halfway and cracking the lid (AWAY from you) to let steam escape as you blend on low speed.

sage to the paper towels to drain and season with salt. Pass the garlic-sage-oil remaining in the skillet through a fine-mesh strainer into a small heatproof bowl.

8   Position an oven rack about 6 inches from the broiler heat source and preheat the broiler.

9   Arrange the baguette slices in a single layer on a baking sheet and brush both sides with olive oil. Broil for a couple of minutes, flipping once, until golden and toasty. The timing will depend on your broiler, so watch the whole time to keep the bread from burning.

10   Ladle the soup into bowls. Top each bowl with a spoonful of the garlic-sage oil, some garlic chips, and some crispy fried sage. Serve with the toasted baguette slices alongside.

NOTE: If you're using squash, cut it crosswise to separate the bulb from the neck. Cut the bulb in half and scoop out the seeds and slice the neck into 1-inch-thick planks.

Melted Caprese Soup

I have always loved the process of taking a beloved flavor and presenting it in a new and exciting way. For years, that was my secret formula for a viral video. Let me give you a peek inside my process: You already know I am a soup girlie. For this particular recipe I was playing around with one of my favorites, French onion soup. Making FOS can be time consuming, so I wanted to encapsulate the same vibe with new flavors. The next step takes creativity and patience while waiting for that genius to strike. For me it was days later, while making a caprese panini for lunch. *That* was that magical flavor combo I was looking for. Each element is perfectly accounted for here, from the roasted tomato soup base to the melted mozzarella atop a floating crostini to the fresh and simmered basil bringing it all together.

SERVES 4

6 Roma (plum) tomatoes, halved

4 tablespoons extra-virgin olive oil, plus more for brushing

Kosher salt and freshly ground black pepper

2 tablespoons unsalted butter

1 large yellow onion, diced

3 garlic cloves, minced or grated

2 tablespoons tomato paste

2 cups low-sodium vegetable stock or chicken stock, plus more as needed

¼ cup finely chopped fresh basil leaves, plus more for serving

1 teaspoon dried oregano

½ cup heavy cream

⅓ cup freshly grated Parmigiano Reggiano cheese, plus more for serving

8 (½-inch-thick) slices baguette, or 4 slices French bread

4 slices fresh mozzarella cheese

Balsamic glaze, for drizzling

1 Preheat the oven to 400°F. Line a baking sheet with aluminum foil.

2 Place the tomatoes cut-side down on the prepared baking sheet. Drizzle with 2 tablespoons of the olive oil and season with salt and pepper. Bake for 35 to 40 minutes, until the tomatoes are lightly charred.

3 In a large pot, heat the remaining 2 tablespoons olive oil with the butter over medium heat. When the butter has melted, add the onion and cook, stirring occasionally, until soft and translucent, about 7 minutes. Add the garlic and cook until fragrant, 1 minute more. Add the tomato paste and cook, stirring often and scraping the bottom of the pot, until the color (and flavors!) deepen, 2 to 3 minutes.

4 Pour in the roasted tomatoes and any juices on the baking sheet, then add the stock and stir, scraping up any browned bits from the bottom of the pot. Stir in the basil and oregano. Bring the soup to a simmer, cover, and cook for 15 to 20 minutes to allow the flavors to meld.

5 Remove the pot from the heat and use an immersion blender to blend the soup directly in the pot until smooth (see Hot Tip, page 68). Add the cream and Parm, and stir to combine. Add more stock if the soup is too thick for you. Simmer, uncovered, until warmed through, 4 to 5 minutes. Taste and season with salt and pepper to your liking.

6 Position an oven rack about 6 inches from the broiler heat source and preheat the broiler. Arrange the baguette slices in a single layer on a baking sheet and brush both sides with olive oil. Broil until golden brown and toasted, just a few minutes on each side (the timing will depend on your broiler, so don't walk away!). Remove the baking sheet from the oven and top each toast with mozzarella.

Broiling means the heat is EXTRA HOT. So if you can't handle the heat . . . STAY IN THE KITCHEN and keep an eye on your oven so nothing burns. Because it will, real fast!

7   Ladle the soup into individual oven-safe bowls or ramekins and place a mozzarella-topped toast on top of each bowl. Place the bowls on the now-empty baking sheet. Slide the baking sheet under the broiler and broil for just a few minutes (watch carefully to prevent burning!), until the cheese is melted and golden. Remove from the oven.

8   Drizzle with balsamic glaze and sprinkle with more basil and Parm. Serve immediately and enjoy!

SALADS, SOUPS & SANDYS   71

Garlic Bread Soup

Cooking is alchemy, the art of transformation. As the story goes, an alchemist turns lead into gold. La-di-da, what does this have to do with garlic? Bear with me. Raw garlic will slap you in the face, much like the many challenges we face in life. Yet under the right conditions, with heat, and pressure, garlic transforms into something almost unrecognizable. This velvety soup is subtly sweet, incredibly luscious, and has a depth that will make you admire what this garlic has been through. Toasted bread is added and, once blended, it thickens the soup like life thickens your skin. While this soup may not hold the same market value as gold, let it remind you that we, too, can transmute stinky moments into golden opportunities.

SERVES 4 AS A MAIN

4 heads garlic

4 tablespoons extra-virgin olive oil, plus more as needed

6 ounces rustic bread (day-old is best!), cut into 1-inch cubes

1 large yellow onion, diced

2 teaspoons ground turmeric

Kosher salt and freshly cracked pepper

4 cups low-sodium chicken stock or vegetable stock

½ cup heavy cream

1 bay leaf

1 teaspoon dried thyme

¼ teaspoon red pepper flakes (optional)

2 tablespoons chopped fresh chives, for serving

Freshly grated Parmigiano Reggiano cheese, for serving

HOT TIP

DO NOT SQUEEZE ROASTED GARLIC STRAIGHT FROM THE OVEN. I LEARNED THIS THE HARD WAY. THIS IS A LITERAL HOT TIP.

1 Preheat the oven to 400°F.

2 Slice about ¼ inch off the top of the garlic heads to expose the cloves. Drizzle with a little olive oil and wrap each head in aluminum foil. Place the wrapped garlic on a baking sheet and roast for 30 to 50 minutes, until the garlic is soft and caramelized. Remove from the oven and let the garlic sit until cool enough to handle (see Hot Tip). Leave the oven on.

3 Place the bread cubes on the same baking sheet, drizzle with 2 tablespoons of the olive oil, and toss to coat. Bake for about 15 minutes, tossing halfway through, until golden brown and toasted.

4 Meanwhile, heat the remaining 2 tablespoons olive oil in a large pot over medium heat. When the oil is shimmering, add the onion and cook, stirring occasionally, until soft and translucent, 7 to 10 minutes. Squeeze the roasted garlic cloves out of their skins and add them to the pot with the onion. Stir well to combine. Add the turmeric, season with salt and pepper, and stir to coat. Cook, stirring continuously, for 1 minute to infuse the flavors. Add the stock, cream, bay leaf, thyme, and red pepper flakes (if using). Increase the heat to high and bring the mixture to a boil, then reduce the heat to low and simmer, uncovered, for 15 to 20 minutes to allow the flavors to meld.

5 Add half the croutons to the soup and simmer until they've softened, 5 minutes. Remove the pot from the heat. Cover and let the soup stand for 10 to 15 minutes so the bread can soak up all the delicious flavors. Discard the bay leaf.

6 Use an immersion blender to puree the soup directly in the pot until smooth (see Hot Tip, page 68), or leave some chunks of bread, if preferred. Taste and adjust the seasoning to your liking. Ladle the soup into bowls, garnish with the remaining croutons, the chives, and freshly grated Parm. Serve right away.

Freekeh-Leek Soup

They say chicken soup is for the soul, and this one happens to match up with mine—it's for the freaks, the geeks, and the freak-a-leeks alike. Zoya and I threw this soup together on a rainy day years ago, and it's become a staple in our house, regardless of the weather. We swapped out noodles for a more regal grain, freekeh, and livened up the flavors with spices, herbs, and lemon. It lives up to its name, so get those juices (meaning chicken stock) flowin', and get ready to get a little FREEKEH!

SERVES 6

2 tablespoons extra-virgin olive oil, plus more for drizzling

2 tablespoons unsalted butter

1 medium yellow onion, diced

4 garlic cloves, minced or grated

Kosher salt

2 leeks, white and light green parts only, sliced and cleaned (see Hot Tip, page 236)

1 teaspoon ground turmeric

¼ teaspoon cayenne pepper

Freshly ground black pepper

1 cup freekeh or farro, rinsed and drained

1 small head cauliflower, chopped into bite-size florets

8 cups low-sodium chicken stock

Juice of ½ lemon, plus more as needed

1 bunch dill, finely chopped

½ bunch cilantro, finely chopped

½ bunch parsley, finely chopped

2 cups shredded rotisserie chicken

For Serving

Labneh or sour cream

Crispy fried onions, store-bought or homemade (see page 234)

Flaky salt

1   In a large pot, heat 1 tablespoon of the olive oil with 1 tablespoon of the butter over medium heat. When the butter has melted, add the onion and cook, stirring occasionally, until soft and translucent, about 7 minutes. Add the garlic and a pinch of salt and cook until soft and fragrant, about 2 minutes.

2   Add the remaining 1 tablespoon olive oil and 1 tablespoon butter. When the butter has melted, add the leeks. Add the turmeric and cayenne and season with pepper and additional salt. Cook, stirring occasionally, until the leeks are soft, 4 to 5 minutes. Add the freekeh and cook, stirring occasionally, until toasted, 2 to 3 minutes. Add the cauliflower, stock, and lemon juice and stir so the vegetables are submerged in the stock. Increase the heat to high and bring the soup to a boil, then reduce the heat to low to maintain a gentle simmer. Cover and cook until the cauliflower and freekeh are tender and cooked through but the freekeh still has a bit of chew, 25 to 30 minutes. Remove the pot from the heat.

3   Add most of the fresh herbs, reserving some for garnish, and use an immersion blender to blend the soup directly in the pot until smooth (see Hot Tip, page 68). Add the chicken and pulse a few times to incorporate it into the soup. Taste and adjust the seasoning to your liking with more salt, pepper, and/or lemon juice.

4   Ladle the soup into bowls and top with a dollop of labneh and a drizzle of olive oil. Sprinkle with the reserved herbs, some fried onions, and flaky salt, and enjoy!

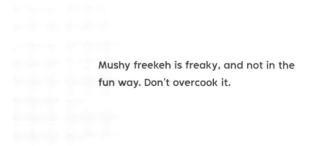

Mushy freekeh is freaky, and not in the fun way. Don't overcook it.

Loaded Chicken Tortilla Soup

I've never related to the saying "less is more." I am a "more is more" kinda gal. More laughter, more fun, more color, more love, more butter. In a world where we are expected to ask for less, we must demand more, and this loaded chicken tortilla soup is the perfect place to start. It has ALL the good stuff and more (except maybe butter): tender chicken, crunchy tortilla strips, queso fresco, avocado, and mouth-watering spices, to name a few. This soup doesn't stay small, and I love that about her. After all, there's nothing wrong with embracing delicious excess—life is too short to be bland.

SERVES 6 TO 8

¼ cup extra-virgin olive oil

1 medium yellow onion, diced

3 garlic cloves, minced or grated

1 small jalapeño, seeded and diced

1 to 2 teaspoons chipotle chile powder

1 to 2 teaspoons ground cumin

1 (15-ounce) can chopped tomatoes, with their juices

8 cups low-sodium chicken stock

¼ cup vegetable oil

10 small (4-inch) corn tortillas, sliced into thin strips

Kosher salt

3 cups shredded rotisserie chicken

1 (15-ounce) can black beans, drained and rinsed

1 (15-ounce) bag frozen corn

Toppings

Crumbled queso fresco

Sliced cabbage

Sliced or diced avocado

Crema or sour cream

Fresh cilantro

Lime wedges

1   Heat the olive oil in a large pot over medium heat. When the oil is shimmering, add the onion, garlic, and jalapeño and cook, stirring occasionally, until the onion is soft and translucent, about 7 minutes. Add the chipotle powder and cumin to taste and cook until the spices are toasted, 1 minute. Add the tomatoes and their juices and cook, stirring occasionally, just to heat them through, 2 minutes. Add 1 cup of the stock and bring the mixture to a boil. Remove from the heat and let the soup base cool slightly.

2   Heat the vegetable oil in a separate medium skillet over medium heat. Line a plate with paper towels. When the oil is shimmering, add 2 or 3 of the tortilla strips; they should immediately bubble—if not, let the oil heat for a few minutes more, then test again. Add the rest of the tortilla strips to the hot oil and cook, stirring often, until crispy and beginning to turn golden, about 5 minutes. Use a slotted spoon or tongs to transfer the tortilla strips to the paper towels to drain. Season with salt.

3   Use an immersion blender to blend the soup base directly in the pot until smooth (see Hot Tip, page 68). Add the remaining 7 cups stock and bring to a boil over medium heat. Add the chicken, black beans, and corn. Taste and season with more salt to your liking. Reduce the heat to maintain a simmer and cook for a few minutes to warm everything through.

4   Place your toppings, including the fried tortilla strips, in individual serving bowls and set them on the table. Ladle the soup into bowls and let everyone top their own.

If you don't feel like making your own chips, just use store-bought. I promise I won't have a chip on my shoulder.

Triple Pickle
Fried Chicken Sandwich

Most of the time, I don't name a recipe until the method of making it has been perfected—rarely does it happen the other way around. This sandwich was one of those exceptions. Truthfully, I don't have much to say about it other than that I love the sound of "triple pickle" (say that five times fast). It's such a great title that I was worried the sandwich itself wouldn't live up to the bold and briny promise its name holds. But it did, it does, and I learned triple the pickles means triple the fun.

SERVES 4

Pickle Aioli

½ cup mayonnaise

1 tablespoon finely chopped dill pickle, plus 2 tablespoons dill pickle brine

1 garlic clove, minced or grated

1 teaspoon Dijon mustard

Kosher salt and freshly ground black pepper

Pickle-Battered Fried Chicken

Vegetable oil, for frying

2 cups all-purpose flour

1 cup dill pickle brine

1 teaspoon sweet paprika

1 teaspoon garlic powder

½ teaspoon kosher salt

¼ teaspoon freshly ground black pepper

¼ teaspoon cayenne pepper

4 boneless, skinless chicken thighs

Sandwiches

1 tablespoon unsalted butter

4 brioche buns

4 butter lettuce leaves

Sliced dill pickles

Tomato slices

½ small red onion, thinly sliced

1 **Make the aioli.** In a small bowl, stir together the mayonnaise, chopped pickle, pickle brine, garlic, and mustard. Season with salt and pepper. Cover and refrigerate for at least 30 minutes or up to overnight.

2 **Make the fried chicken.** Fill a large pot with about 3 inches of oil. Clip a deep-fry thermometer to the side of the pan and heat the oil over medium-high heat until it reaches 350°F (see Hot Tip). Set a wire rack over a baking sheet or line a plate with paper towels.

3 In a shallow dish, whisk together 1 cup of the flour, the pickle brine, paprika, garlic powder, salt, black pepper, and cayenne until the batter is smooth. Place the remaining 1 cup flour in a separate shallow dish.

4 Working with one piece at a time, dip each chicken thigh in the flour to coat, shaking off any excess, then dip it into the batter, turning to coat and letting any excess drip off. Carefully place the battered chicken in the hot oil and repeat with another piece. Cook until the chicken is golden brown and cooked through—it should register 165°F on an instant-read thermometer—5 to 8 minutes per side. Transfer the fried chicken to the rack to drain. Repeat to batter and fry the remaining chicken thighs, allowing the oil to return to temperature between batches.

5 **Assemble the sandwiches.** Melt the butter in a large cast-iron skillet over medium-high heat, tilting the pan to coat the bottom. Add the buns cut-side down and toast until golden brown, about 3 minutes. Transfer to a plate.

6 Spread a layer of the pickle aioli over each bottom bun. Place some lettuce, dill pickles, and a fried chicken thigh on top and finish with tomato and onion. Serve while crispy and hot!

If you're frying, plan on buying . . . a thermometer. Seriously, the right temperature is crucial: If your oil is too cool, your coating will be soggy; if it's too hot, the breading will burn before the chicken cooks through.

Kookoo Sandwich

Once upon a time, Persian cuisine and I were like two star-crossed lovers, worlds apart. But thanks to the culinary cupid that is my partner, Zoya, I've fallen head over heels for Persian food. Out of love and respect for her culture, and because selfishly I want to be eatin' good, I've spent a lot of time learning how to cook the Persian classics. This one in particular is a delicious fusion of my two greatest loves: Persian food and sandwiches (sorry, Zoya!). Persian cooking layers flavors and textures like no other, with tons of fresh herbs, spices, and acidity. Kookoo sabzi is vaguely similar to an egg frittata, packed full of fragrant herbs, sour barberries, and crunchy walnuts. Eat it sandwiched between fluffy bread, filled with more yummy toppings. I'm confident you'll be cuckoo for kookoo, just like me.

SERVES 4

Kookoo Sabzi

8 ounces (2 to 3 bunches) parsley

8 ounces (2 to 3 bunches) cilantro

2 ounces (about 1 bunch) dill

4 to 6 large eggs, as needed

¼ cup all-purpose flour

1 teaspoon baking powder

Kosher salt and freshly ground black pepper

2 small bunches scallions, thinly sliced

¼ cup walnuts, coarsely chopped

2 tablespoons dried barberries or currants, rinsed (optional)

2 tablespoons vegetable oil

Sandwiches

½ cup labneh

2 tablespoons finely chopped fresh dill, plus more for serving

Juice of ½ lemon, plus more if needed

Kosher salt and freshly ground black pepper

4 flatbreads (pita, lavash, or 8 slices of whatever bread you have, like barbari)

Sliced tomatoes

Sliced pickles

Thinly sliced red onion

Crumbled feta cheese

1 Make the kookoo. Pick the leaves from the parsley, cilantro, and dill. Finely chop the herbs, either by hand or in batches in a food processor—there will be a lot of them and it'll take some time, but the end result will be worth it!

2 In a large bowl, whisk 4 eggs until smooth. Add the flour and baking powder and season generously with salt and pepper. Whisk until smooth. Add all the chopped herbs, the scallions, walnuts, and barberries (if using). Fold until well combined. The batter should be very thick and all the ingredients just barely coated in egg. If necessary, add more eggs one at a time, mixing after each, until it is.

3 Heat the vegetable oil in a large nonstick skillet over medium heat. When the oil is shimmering, pour in the egg mixture, spreading it evenly to the edges in with your spatula. Immediately run the spatula through the mixture to divide it into quarters for easier flipping, repeating this action continuously so the quarters separate as they set. Cook, rotating the pan regularly, until the bottoms are browned, 5 to 7 minutes. Flip each quarter over and cook until golden brown and cooked through, adjusting the heat if it browns too quickly, 4 to 5 minutes. Transfer to a plate.

4 Make the sandwiches. In a small bowl, stir together the labneh, dill, and lemon juice and season with salt and pepper. Taste and adjust the seasoning to your liking.

5 Spread each flatbread with a generous amount of the labneh sauce. Place a piece of kookoo sabzi on the labneh sauce and layer with tomatoes, pickles, and onion, then sprinkle with dill and feta. Enjoy right away!

Take a cue from Missy Elliot: Put your thing (the spatula) down, flip it (the kookoo), and reverse it (cook the other side) in one swift motion so the only thing we're dropping to the floor is ourselves.

BBQ Steak & Fried Onion Sandwich

Calling all big boys and big girls. This one's for you. A mouthwatering, tear-jerking monster of a sandwich so hefty, it requires clear eyes, full hearts, and two hands. Bring your biggest, hungriest appetite and a can't-lose attitude. With steak so juicy it oozes and fried onions that add a crispy, flavorful crunch, you're going to need to grab a napkin and unbutton your jeans.

SERVES 4

¼ cup your favorite barbecue sauce, plus more for serving

2 tablespoons extra-virgin olive oil

1 tablespoon Worcestershire sauce

1 teaspoon garlic powder

1 teaspoon onion powder

¾ teaspoon smoked paprika

Kosher salt and freshly ground black pepper

1 pound rib eye, sirloin, or flank steak, about 1 inch thick

Vegetable oil, for frying

½ cup all-purpose flour

1 large yellow onion, thinly sliced

For Serving

Mayonnaise or your preferred sandwich condiment

8 slices of your favorite crusty bread (ciabatta and sourdough work well)

Sliced tomatoes

Arugula

Lemon wedges, for squeezing

1 In a small bowl, whisk together the barbecue sauce, olive oil, Worcestershire, garlic powder, onion powder, and ½ teaspoon of the paprika. Season generously with salt and pepper. Place the steak in a resealable plastic bag or a shallow dish and pour the marinade over it, turning to coat. Seal the bag or cover the dish and marinate in the refrigerator for at least 2 hours or preferably overnight.

2 Fill a large deep skillet or pot with about 2 inches of oil. Clip a deep-fry thermometer to the side of the pan and heat the oil over medium-high heat until it reaches 375°F (see Hot Tip, page 79). Line a plate with paper towels.

3 Meanwhile, heat a large cast-iron skillet over medium-high heat. When the pan is hot and smoking, remove the steak from the marinade and shake off any excess. Cook the steak, flipping regularly for even browning, until it reaches 135°F for medium-rare, about 10 minutes total, or adjust the cooking time for your preferred doneness (for medium, go for another 3 minutes or so until it's 145°F; or about 3 minutes less, to 125°F, for rare). Transfer the steak to a plate and let it rest for 10 minutes.

4 While the steak rests, in a shallow bowl, stir together the flour and remaining ¼ teaspoon paprika and season with salt and pepper. Dip the onion slices into the flour mixture, tossing to coat evenly, and shake off any excess flour. Working in batches, add the coated onion slices to the hot oil and cook until golden and crispy, 2 to 4 minutes. Use a slotted spoon to transfer the fried onions to the paper towel–lined plate to drain. Season with a pinch of salt. Repeat with the remaining onion slices, allowing the oil to return to temperature between batches.

HOT TIP

My best advice to you is to go against the grain, both in life and in slicing steak.

5 Thinly slice the steak against the grain. Spread some mayonnaise and barbecue sauce on each piece of bread. Arrange the tomato slices on 4 slices of bread. Layer the steak on the tomatoes, dividing it evenly, and top with fried onions and arugula. Squeeze some lemon juice over the arugula. Close each sandwich and serve.

FAKE IT TILL YOU BAKE IT

While I don't love the phrase "fake it till you make it," there's truth to it. To me, it's not about being *fake*, but about pushing through the belief that you can't do something because you don't have the skills to. Spoiler alert! Most people don't know what they're doing—successful people just don't let that stop them. Take it from me: I studied science in college, never went to culinary school, and definitely didn't go to film school. In fact, when I was hired as an intern at Tasty, I'd never even made a video (not counting the fake music videos I made with friends after school). So how did I end up with a thriving career as a food video producer? I simply believed in my ability to learn.

Just weeks before graduating college, I realized I didn't want the nursing career I'd been preparing for. Nursing was the responsible choice, but I've never been one to follow the beaten path. I'd already started a food blog as a hobby. I probably had five viewers, two of whom were my parents, but those five were enough to give me the confidence to change the course of my life.

After graduation, I bought myself some time—one year—and moved to Sweden. I had never been to Scandinavia before, but I made a pact with myself that if I didn't end up making it big as a food blogger in that one year, I would move back and get that hospital job. (Can you imagine clumsy ME in a hospital?! PHEW.) I worked as an au pair, living with a family in an apartment in Stockholm. I had some free time while the kids were at school, so I blogged during the day and looked for a side job to keep me busy. I found the phone number a prominent Swedish food writer,

Mia Gahne, and I called it. It was a bold move but must have been fate because her assistant had quit the day before. To my surprise, she hired me on the spot as her new assistant food stylist.

It was a dream—and I owe Mia a lot. We would cook alongside each other in a studio kitchen by the water. She had a rustic style and made the most beautiful food so effortlessly. We cooked, ate, drank, laughed, and talked. Time would fly by, and I often had to run to the bus stop in the afternoon so I wouldn't be late to pick up the kids. It was the first time I felt like I had a place in the food world.

What stuck with me most was how Mia trusted me—a random American girl in Sweden with nothing to offer but a food blog with five viewers. One day, while we were cooking, I felt off, nervous that I was getting it all wrong. I kept asking Mia questions about a recipe until she finally turned to me and said, "Alix, stop asking me questions. You know what you are doing. Trust yourself." That dose of tough love was a lightbulb moment. Confidence is not something you're given—it's something you own. And it's always within.

Life has a way of presenting us with the right people and experiences at the perfect time to move us toward our purpose. If you're living in alignment with your purpose, you've made it. Simple as that. Oh, and about that little pact: Just a month shy of my one-year anniversary in Sweden, I bought a one-way ticket from Stockholm to Los Angeles, to start my internship at BuzzFeed Tasty.

Little did I know, I was about to make it.

THREE

DIPS, SNACKS, AND APPS

Potato Chip Onion Rings

Developing a recipe for the visual internet is interesting because it has to be exciting enough to keep you watching the video and delicious enough to get you to want to cook. It has to be accessible so it can reach the masses, yet unique. Making a viral recipe video can be a bit like throwing spaghetti at a wall, but every so often I would think something I just knew would be a hit. Like this one: onion rings coated in crushed-up flavored potato chips and fried until beautifully golden, the perfect marriage of flavors that will have you singing "PUT A RING ON IT." I like to use Lay's because they're thin and make the best crumbs. A trio of flavors like Original, BBQ, and Sour Cream & Onion is so good. Make each flavor or go crazy and mix them to make your own Franken-flavor. As always, feel free to get fun and funky with what you choose!

Serves 4 to 8

Vegetable oil, for frying

15 ounces any flavor Lay's potato chips

1 cup all-purpose flour

1 teaspoon kosher salt, plus more as needed

1 teaspoon freshly ground black pepper, plus more as needed

3 large eggs

¼ cup buttermilk

2 large yellow or white onions

Finely chopped fresh parsley, for serving

Dipping sauces of your choice, for serving

Use two hands when dredging, keeping one for the wet ingredients and one for the dry, or your fingers will end up with a thick coating of their own.

1   Fill a large Dutch oven or heavy-bottomed pot with about 2 inches of oil, or enough to come halfway up the sides. Clip a deep-fry thermometer to the side of the pot and heat the oil over medium-high heat until it reaches 375°F (see Hot Tip, page 79). Set a wire rack over a baking sheet.

2   Place the potato chips in a resealable plastic bag (keep the flavors separate if you're using more than one) and crush them into crumbs—think coarse enough to have some texture but fine enough to stick. Transfer to a shallow bowl. Place the flour in a separate shallow bowl, add the salt and pepper, and mix to combine. Break the eggs into a third shallow bowl, add the buttermilk and a pinch each of salt and pepper, and whisk to combine. Place another baking sheet next to your work area.

3   Slice the onions into ¾-inch-thick rings and separate the individual layers. Set aside the nice, big outer rings and reserve the smaller center rings for another use.

4   Using one hand, dredge an onion ring in the flour mixture, pressing to coat and shaking off any excess. Using the other hand, dip the onion ring in the egg mixture to coat, allowing any excess to drip off. Dip it once more in the flour, then in the egg. Dip the onion ring in the chip crumbs to coat thoroughly, then set the breaded onion ring on the baking sheet. Repeat with the remaining onion rings, or until you run out of dredging ingredients.

5   Working in batches, add the onion rings to the hot oil and cook until golden brown all over, about 2 minutes. They'll cook quickly, so watch them carefully and adjust the heat as needed to keep the oil temperature steady. Use a slotted spoon to transfer the onion rings to the wire rack to drain. Salt them, if you like. Repeat with the remaining onion rings, allowing the oil to return to temperature between batches.

6   Sprinkle the onion rings with parsley and serve hot, with your favorite sauces alongside for dipping.

Smashburger Sliders

I have only one question here: SMASH OR PASS? I highly suggest you smash.

Makes 12

Burger Sauce

½ cup mayonnaise

¼ cup ketchup

¼ cup Dijon mustard

2 tablespoons honey, plus more as needed

2 tablespoons pickle relish

2 tablespoons apple cider vinegar

1 tablespoon sriracha

1 tablespoon garlic powder

½ teaspoon onion powder

Kosher salt and freshly ground black pepper

Smashburgers

1 pound ground beef (I like 80/20 grass-fed)

Extra-virgin olive oil, for greasing

2 tablespoons unsalted butter

Kosher salt and freshly ground black pepper

3 slices yellow American cheese, cut into quarters

12 Hawaiian rolls, split

½ medium yellow onion, finely diced

Pickle slices, for serving

You might have to scrape the smashed patty off the pan to flip it, which can be hard if your patty is too thin. Smash with care, take your time, and be sure to get all those crusty bits off—that's the GOOD stuff.

1   Make the burger sauce. In a medium bowl, stir together the mayonnaise, ketchup, mustard, honey, pickle relish, apple cider vinegar, and sriracha until well combined. Add the garlic powder and onion powder and season with salt and pepper to your liking. Stir again to incorporate. Taste and adjust the sweetness by adding more honey, if desired. Cover and refrigerate the burger sauce for at least 30 minutes or up to overnight to allow the flavors to meld. The recipe makes plenty and it will keep in the fridge for at least 1 week!

2   Make the smashburgers. Heat a large cast-iron skillet or griddle over medium-high heat. Cut twelve 4-inch-ish squares of parchment paper for the burgers.

3   Divide the ground beef into 12 equal portions and shape them into small balls. Brush the skillet or griddle with some olive oil, then melt the butter in the skillet. Working with one piece at a time, place a ground beef ball on the hot pan and top with a square of parchment paper. Immediately press down with a flat spatula to smash the beef into a patty wide enough that you have plenty of surface area, but not so thin that you can't flip it. Remove the parchment. Repeat the smashing process with as many ground beef balls as will fit in the pan, being sure not to crowd them. Season the patties with salt and pepper and cook until they develop a nice crust on the bottom, 1 to 2 minutes. Flip and cook to your desired level of doneness, about 2 minutes more. In the last 30 seconds of cooking, place a quarter slice of cheese on top of each and cover the pan with a lid so the cheese melts. Transfer the sliders to a plate. Repeat with the remaining beef and cheese.

4   Spread some sauce on the bottom half of each slider bun. Place a smashburger patty on each bottom bun. Top the patties with some onion, a couple of pickle slices, and the top buns, and enjoy.

Melted Shallot Dip

I think of shallots as the charming, sweeter siblings of onions. They might not be as loud, but it's time to pass them the mic, because the shallots have something to SAY! We are melting them into creamy perfection here, and adding layers of spice, acid, and fat to amplify their subtle sophistication. Like French onion dip, but fancier. If you want to try out my preferred delivery vessel, grab a chip and take a dip. And be quick about it—this is always the first thing to disappear from the table. Pro tip: The bigger the shallots, the fewer you have to peel.

Makes 3 cups

2 tablespoons unsalted butter

1 pound shallots, thinly sliced

1 teaspoon sherry vinegar

Kosher salt

Big pinch of sugar

2 cups sour cream or labneh

¼ cup mayonnaise (optional)

½ teaspoon garlic powder

½ teaspoon onion powder

¼ teaspoon cayenne pepper (optional)

Freshly ground black pepper

1 tablespoon finely chopped fresh chives, for garnish

Sturdy potato chips, for serving

1 Melt the butter in a medium skillet over medium heat. Add the shallots and cook, stirring often, until they are soft and beginning to take on some color, 5 to 7 minutes. Add the vinegar, a big pinch of salt, and the sugar.

2 Reduce the heat to medium-low, cover the pan, and cook, stirring occasionally and adjusting the heat as needed to prevent burning, until the shallots are caramelized and golden brown in color, 15 to 20 minutes more. Remove from the heat and let cool for a few minutes. Taste and adjust the seasoning to your liking, then transfer to a medium bowl.

3 Add the sour cream, mayonnaise (if using), garlic powder, onion powder, and cayenne (if using). Season with black pepper and stir to combine well. Taste and adjust the seasoning to your liking.

4 Transfer the shallot dip to a serving bowl, cover, and refrigerate for at least 1 hour or, even better, up to 24 hours before serving to allow the flavors to meld and the dip to thicken.

5 Remove the dip from the fridge and allow it to sit at room temperature for a few minutes to soften and warm slightly before serving. Sprinkle with the chives and serve with potato chips for dipping.

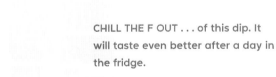

CHILL THE F OUT . . . of this dip. It will taste even better after a day in the fridge.

Whipped Feta Tzatziki
WITH TOMATO CONFIT

This dip has got me wrapped around its finger, or shall I say: It has me whipped. Something I love about food is its ability to instantly transport you with one bite. With this dip, we are island hopping in the Mediterranean, where the cool and classic tzatziki marries the rich and velvety whipped feta. It's my version of a Big Fat Greek Wedding. The confit is just the cherry (tomatoes) on top, but you can skip it if you're rushing down the aisle.

Serves 4 to 6

1 cup small cherry tomatoes, stemmed if needed

½ cup plus 2 tablespoons extra-virgin olive oil, plus more as needed

1 sprig oregano, plus more for serving

½ teaspoon red pepper flakes

Kosher salt and freshly ground black pepper

1 English cucumber, or 3 Persian cucumbers

1 (8-ounce) block feta cheese, crumbled

2 tablespoons coarsely chopped fresh dill

2 garlic cloves, coarsely chopped

Juice of ½ lemon, plus more as needed

1 cup labneh or plain full-fat Greek yogurt

For Serving

Flaky salt

Red pepper flakes (optional)

Pita bread, pita chips, or vegetable crudités

Precrumbled feta = JAIL. Opt for the good stuff sold in brine—it should be wet, not dry.

1 Combine the tomatoes, ½ cup of the olive oil, the oregano, and the red pepper flakes in a small saucepan and season with salt and black pepper. If the tomatoes aren't completely submerged, add more oil as needed to cover. Cook over medium-low heat until bubbles begin to rise to the surface. Reduce the heat to low so there are only a few bubbles and cook, undisturbed, adjusting the heat as needed to maintain consistent bubbling, until the tomatoes soften and begin to collapse and split, about 20 minutes. Remove from the heat and let the tomatoes sit in the warm oil to soften further while you make the dip.

2 Grate the cucumber on the largest holes of a box grater. Using your hands and working over the sink or a bowl, squeeze out as much of the moisture as you can, discard the liquid, and measure out 1 cup of the grated cucumber (reserve the remainder for another use).

3 In a food processor or blender, combine the feta, dill, garlic, and lemon juice and season with salt and black pepper. Process until smooth and creamy, creating a whipped texture. With the motor running, drizzle in the remaining 2 tablespoons olive oil and process to incorporate it. Taste and adjust the seasoning to your liking with more salt, black pepper, and/or lemon juice.

4 Transfer the whipped feta to a serving bowl. Fold in the labneh and grated cucumber. Taste and adjust the seasoning one more time. Use a slotted spoon to top the dip with the tomatoes and then add a drizzle of the tomato oil from the pan. Sprinkle with more oregano, some flaky salt, and red pepper flakes, if desired. Serve with pita bread for dipping.

Cheesy Artichoke Dip

This recipe is courtesy of my best friend Sydney Surprise and her mom, Kathy. Sydney and I met freshman year of college when we lived in the same dorm. When we discovered we were from the same hometown and both had English bulldogs, and, strangely, that I had attended her high school graduation (I know because I don't forget a name like Sydney Surprise), we became best friends fast. During holidays and breaks, we would travel home together, and this dip was always the first thing we asked her mom to make for us. You might notice artichokes' usual sidekick spinach is missing—that's no mistake. This dip puts the spotlight on the artichokes; its beauty is in its simplicity—and ample dairy.

Serves 8 to 10

1 cup sour cream

1 cup mayonnaise

1 (8-ounce) block cream cheese, at room temperature

2 (14-ounce) cans artichoke bottoms or hearts, drained and chopped

2 garlic cloves, minced or grated

2 cups freshly grated Parmigiano Reggiano cheese

Sliced crusty bread or your favorite crackers, for serving

1   Preheat the oven to 400°F.

2   In a large bowl, stir together the sour cream, mayonnaise, and cream cheese until smooth and well combined. Add the artichokes, garlic, and 1 cup of the Parm and stir to incorporate them. Transfer to a 9×12-inch baking dish and top evenly with the remaining 1 cup Parm.

3   Bake for about 20 minutes, until the cheese is melted and the dip is bubbling. Switch the oven to broil and cook for 2 to 3 minutes more, until the cheese is golden and browned in spots. Enjoy immediately with bread or crackers!

I have no tip for this dip. You really can't mess it up.

Nachos Supreme Dip

I will never have people over to my house without putting out food for them to eat. I once made this dip for a party ten minutes before people arrived, based solely on the ingredients in my fridge and the knowledge that all my friends love Taco Bell (the key to being a good host is knowing your guests better than they know themselves). Well, let me tell you, the party revolved around the table this dip was sitting on, and when it was all gone, the conversation revolved around its memory. Like deconstructed nachos that ensure you get all the best parts in every single bite, this dip is definitely supreme.

Serves 6 to 8

2 tablespoons extra-virgin olive oil

1 medium yellow onion, diced

2 garlic cloves, minced or grated

1 pound ground beef (I like 80/20 grass-fed)

1 (1-ounce) packet taco seasoning (see Hot Tip)

1 (15-ounce) can refried beans

2 cups shredded Mexican cheese blend

1 cup sour cream, plus more as needed

1 large tomato, diced and drained

1 (2.25-ounce) can sliced black olives, drained

¼ cup crumbled queso fresco

¼ cup fresh cilantro

2 scallions, sliced

Thick tortilla chips, for serving

1   Preheat the oven to 400°F.

2   Heat the olive oil in a large skillet over medium heat. When the oil is shimmering, add the onion and cook, stirring occasionally, until soft and translucent, about 7 minutes. Add the garlic and cook until fragrant, 1 minute. Add the ground beef and cook, breaking it up with a wooden spoon, until browned and cooked through, 8 to 10 minutes. Sprinkle in the taco seasoning and stir to combine. Remove from the heat.

3   Spread the refried beans evenly over the bottom of a 9×12-inch baking dish. Top with the beef mixture, then sprinkle the shredded cheese over the top.

4   Bake for 15 to 20 minutes, until the cheese is melted and bubbling. Remove from the oven and let cool for 10 minutes.

5   Spread an even layer of sour cream over the dip, covering all the cheese, then top with the tomato and olives. Sprinkle with the queso fresco, cilantro, and scallions. Serve right away, with tortilla chips for dipping.

To DIY taco seasoning, mix 1 tablespoon chili powder with 1 teaspoon each ground cumin, smoked paprika, garlic powder, onion powder, dried oregano, salt, and black pepper.

Elote Fritters

Nothing screams "summer" like corn, and nothing screams "corn" like elote. Elote is all the best things—sweet, creamy, crunchy, salty, tangy—and this recipe gives you an excuse to add "fried" to that list. Now, if you're making this in the summer, you may have access to fresh corn—good for you! Get shucking. I, for one, prefer to use frozen corn because I am lazy. That also means I can make this recipe with great, consistent results year-round. So shuck your cobs or chuck your cobs, because the only things cornier than this recipe are my jokes.

Serves 4

1 cup all-purpose flour

2 teaspoons baking powder

1 teaspoon kosher salt

1 teaspoon chili powder

½ teaspoon freshly ground black pepper

½ teaspoon cayenne pepper, plus more for serving

1 cup seltzer or sparkling water

3 cups frozen corn kernels

4 scallions, thinly sliced

½ cup crumbled Cotija cheese, plus more for serving

¼ cup finely chopped fresh cilantro, plus more for serving

6 to 8 tablespoons unsalted butter, as needed

For Serving

Mayonnaise or sour cream

Flaky salt

Tajín (optional)

Lime wedges

1   In a large bowl, whisk together the flour, baking powder, salt, chili powder, black pepper, and cayenne. Pour in the seltzer and whisk until smooth. Fold in the corn, scallions, Cotija, and cilantro until well combined.

2   Melt 2 tablespoons of the butter in a large cast-iron skillet over medium heat. Line a plate with a paper towel. Scoop ¼-cup portions of the batter into the skillet, flattening each with a spoon and leaving some space between them. Cook until golden brown and cooked through, adjusting the heat if necessary to prevent the butter from burning, about 4 minutes per side. Transfer the fritters to the paper towel to drain. Repeat with the remaining batter, adding more butter to the pan 2 tablespoons at a time between batches.

3   Transfer the fritters to a serving platter and finish with a swipe of mayo, then a sprinkle of flaky salt, Cotija, and more cilantro. If you like spice, sprinkle them with a little Tajín or more cayenne, too. Serve hot, with lime wedges for squeezing, and enjoy!

Always test the waters, or in this case, the fritters. Cook a spoonful of your batter so you can check for seasoning and consistency. If they're underseasoned, add some salt; if they fall apart, add some flour.

Green Goddess Eggs

I know they are a bit polarizing, but I love a deviled egg. If it's wrong, I don't want to be right—at least that's what the little devil on my shoulder tells me. But this is a deviled egg's alter ego, my heavenly version. Picture velvety yolks mixed with an aromatic blend of fresh herbs, giving you a taste so divine, you may just ascend to flavor eggstasy with each bite.

Makes 12

6 large eggs

2 tablespoons sour cream or plain full-fat Greek yogurt

1 tablespoon mayonnaise

1 tablespoon chopped fresh chives, plus more for serving

1 tablespoon chopped fresh parsley

1 tablespoon chopped fresh dill

2 teaspoons drained capers, plus more for serving

2 teaspoons Dijon mustard

1 garlic clove, peeled

½ lemon

Kosher salt and freshly ground black pepper

Flaky salt, for serving

We're going for green eggs . . . because of the herbs, *not* the yolks. Overcooking a hard-boiled egg leads to dry yolks and an unsightly green-grayish color.

1   Fill a medium bowl with ice water and set it near the stove. Place the eggs in a medium saucepan and add water to cover by about 1 inch. Bring the water to a boil over medium-high heat. As soon as it reaches a boil, remove the pot from the heat and cover. Let stand for 14 minutes, then use a slotted spoon to transfer the eggs to the ice water.

2   When the eggs are cool, peel them and halve them lengthwise. Carefully remove the yolks and pop them into a blender or food processor; set the whites aside. Add the sour cream, mayonnaise, chives, parsley, dill, capers, mustard, and garlic to the blender or food processor. Squeeze in some lemon juice and season with salt and pepper. Pulse until smooth and combined, stopping to scrape down the sides as needed; the number of pulses will depend on your machine, but stop when the capers are broken down. Taste and adjust the seasoning to your liking.

3   Transfer the yolk mixture to a piping bag or a resealable plastic bag. (To make this easier, place the bag in a tall glass or container and fold the top of the bag down over the rim of the glass.) Cut ½ inch off the bottom of the piping bag (or from one corner, if using a resealable plastic bag) to pipe a thick ribbon of filling, or cut a narrower opening to pipe a finer ribbon, if you want to get fancy with your designs. Pipe the yolk mixture into each egg white half to fill.

4   Transfer the eggs to a serving plate and sprinkle with more chives, capers, and flaky salt.

Sizzled Scallion–Stuffed Flatbread

There's a reason bread was one of the very first foods made by mankind: because it's good. Each culture has its own variation of flour and water. From naan to pita, barbari to tortillas, I happen to love them all. This quick flatbread is nothing short of magic, coming together with just a few staple ingredients and no messing around with yeast and proofing. Just mix, take a breather, and stuff it with the next best thing after bread: cheese. Boursin is one of my favorite cheeses because it's ultra-creamy and luxurious. Paired with the sizzled scallions, it creates an irresistible filling. If you don't have Boursin, cream cheese would swap in well.

Makes 10

4 cups all-purpose flour, plus more if needed

1 tablespoon baking powder

1 teaspoon kosher salt, plus more as needed

2½ cups plain full-fat Greek yogurt, plus more if needed

2 tablespoons extra-virgin olive oil

½ cup sliced scallions

2 (5.2-ounce) packages Garlic & Fine Herbs Boursin cheese, at room temperature

4 or 5 tablespoons unsalted butter, for greasing

When I am well rested, I'm much less likely to snap back at my partner, and the same goes for dough. Be sure to let it rest after kneading for easy rolling.

1 In a large bowl, whisk together the flour, baking powder, and salt. Add the yogurt and stir with a wooden spoon or spatula until you get a shaggy dough. Using clean hands, bring the dough together into a ball, incorporating any loose bits of flour; the dough should be smooth and tacky, not too wet or too dry. If it's too dry, add a little more yogurt; if it's too wet, add a little more flour. Cover the dough with a clean kitchen towel and let it rest for 20 minutes.

2 Meanwhile, heat the olive oil in a small skillet over medium heat. When the oil is shimmering, add the scallions and a pinch of salt and cook, stirring often, until just softened but not yet colored, about 4 minutes. Place the cheese in a small bowl, pour over the scallions and oil, and stir to combine.

3 On a clean work surface, divide the dough into 10 equal pieces (if the dough is sticky after resting, lightly dust the counter first). Working with one piece at a time, roll the dough between your palms into a ball. Press down to flatten it and then roll it out into a flat, ¼-inch-thick disc (I like to use a chopstick for this), rotating the dough round as you roll to keep the shape even. Scoop 1 heaping tablespoon of the scallion-cheese mixture into the center of the dough round. Bring the edges of the dough together over the filling to form a ball and pinch to close. Place the ball seam-side down and use your palm to flatten it to ½ inch thick. Repeat with the remaining dough and filling.

4 Melt 1 tablespoon of the butter in a large nonstick skillet over medium heat. Working in batches, pop 2 or 3 of the flatbreads into the pan, without crowding, and cook until golden brown and cooked through, 3 to 5 minutes on each side. Transfer to a plate (no need to cover) and repeat with the remaining flatbreads, adding more butter to the pan 1 tablespoon at a time between batches so the pan stays greased, and adjusting the heat if the butter is browning too quickly. Serve immediately and enjoy!

Chili Crisp Chicken Wings

When I was a kid, I wanted so badly to have wings. To this day, when someone asks what superpower I would choose, I say to fly. (The closest I've come is jumping out of a plane in Switzerland, but I don't think free-falling feels quite the same as flying.) I'm not one for settling, but when it comes to wings, I've found these to be the next best thing. They're fiery and crispy, sticky and sweet, and you'll be flying high on flavor with each bite.

Serves 4 to 6

Nonstick cooking spray

2 pounds mixed flats and drumettes or whole chicken wings, halved at the joints, wing tips discarded

1 tablespoon baking powder

1 teaspoon kosher salt

½ teaspoon freshly ground black pepper

¼ cup chili crisp

2 tablespoons honey

Sesame seeds, for serving

Sliced scallions, for serving

1 Position a rack in the center of the oven and preheat to 425°F. Line a baking sheet with aluminum foil and set a wire rack on top, then coat the rack with cooking spray.

2 Pat the wings dry with paper towels and place them in a large bowl. Add the baking powder, salt, and pepper and toss, being sure the wings are all well coated. Place them in a single layer on the prepared rack, leaving some space between each.

3 Bake for 45 to 55 minutes, turning halfway through, until the wings are crispy and browned. Remove from the oven and let cool for a few minutes, then transfer the wings to a large bowl (keep the baking sheet with the rack handy). Switch the oven to broil.

4 Pour the chili crisp and honey over the wings and toss to coat evenly. Return the wings to the wire rack, meaty-side up, and broil for 2 to 3 minutes, until the sauce caramelizes and the wings are extra crispy. Keep a close eye on them to prevent burning!

5 Transfer the wings to a serving platter and sprinkle with sesame seeds and scallions. Serve immediately (with lots of napkins)!

We just want to achieve a little caramelization, so when you get to broiling, don't move the oven rack up to the highest position, or the sugar in the glaze will likely burn.

Crispy Taco Triangles

Tacos come in all shapes and sizes. This version happens to come in triangles. They have a hard and crunchy exterior, but remember, it's what's on the inside that counts, and you can find infinite ways to fill your tacos (and your life) with flavor. Whether you're a meat lover, bean enthusiast, or a chicken-taco purist, choose your fighter and embrace the opportunity to make the filling your own. Just remember my golden rule: Cook your foods the way you like to eat them. Deep-fried.

Makes 20

Vegetable oil, for frying

3 tablespoons extra-virgin olive oil

1 pound ground beef (I like 80/20 grass-fed), or 2 cups shredded rotisserie chicken, drained canned black beans, or refried beans

2 teaspoons kosher salt

1 teaspoon freshly ground black pepper

1 medium yellow onion, sliced

1 red bell pepper, sliced

1 green bell pepper, sliced

1 teaspoon smoked paprika

1 teaspoon chili powder

1 teaspoon ground cumin

1 teaspoon garlic powder

1 teaspoon dried oregano

Juice of 1 lime

1 large egg

10 (12-inch) flour tortillas, cut in half

2 cups shredded Mexican cheese blend

For Serving

Chopped fresh cilantro

Sour cream

Guacamole

Salsa

Want to avoid a taco meltdown? Seal those tortillas right and tight. If they're not snug or you get a little too generous with the filling, your triangles may explode in the oil. Keep the meat neat and the edges sealed, and your tacos will fry up without a hitch!

1 Fill a large Dutch oven or heavy-bottomed pot with 2 inches of vegetable oil. Clip a deep-fry thermometer to the side of the pot and heat the oil over medium-high heat until it reaches 350°F (see Hot Tip, page 79). Set a wire rack over a baking sheet.

2 (If you're using beans or chicken instead of beef, skip to the next step.) Heat 2 tablespoons of the olive oil in a large skillet over medium heat. When the oil is shimmering, add the ground beef and season with 1 teaspoon of the salt and ½ teaspoon of the black pepper. Cook, breaking it up with a wooden spoon, until browned and cooked through, about 15 minutes. Use a slotted spoon to transfer the beef to a large bowl. Discard the fat and wipe out the pan.

3 Return the pan to the stove and heat the remaining 1 tablespoon olive oil over medium heat. When the oil is shimmering, add the onion, red and green bell peppers, paprika, chili powder, cumin, garlic powder, oregano, remaining 1 teaspoon salt, and remaining ½ teaspoon black pepper. Stir to combine. Add the lime juice and cook, stirring occasionally, until the vegetables are soft, about 5 minutes. Add the vegetables to the bowl with the beef (or add your chicken or beans now) and stir to incorporate.

4 Beat the egg in a small bowl. Place ¼ cup of the filling in the center of one tortilla half and sprinkle with 1 tablespoon of the cheese. Fold each corner across the middle and down, overlapping the sides to form a triangle. Brush the seams and bottom opening with the egg and pinch the side seam firmly to seal, then press the bottom opening with a fork to seal. Repeat with the remaining tortillas and fillings.

5 Place 2 or 3 tortilla triangles in the hot oil and cook until golden brown on both sides, about 3 minutes total, adjusting the heat as needed to keep the oil temperature steady. Use tongs to transfer the triangles to the rack to drain. Repeat with the remaining triangles, allowing the oil to return to temperature between batches.

6 While the taco triangles are still hot, garnish with cilantro and serve with sour cream, guacamole, and salsa.

Frickles

I'm calling in all people pleasers with this one, because we can take a cue from pickles. While being universally loved sounds appealing, it often means you're not boldly embracing your true flavors. Playing it safe and small so you'll be liked means you forgo the opportunity to be truly loved. Pickles, like the most authentic and interesting personalities, are polarizing with their unapologetic zing. Whether they're hated for it or loved for it, pickles are going to pickle even if they're a tad extra, and I think that's a beautiful thing. In fact, I say get *extra* extra by frying these gorgeous pickles into crispy, golden, and tangy frickles. That's called a GLOW UP.

Serves 2 to 4

Vegetable oil, for frying

1 cup whole milk

½ cup all-purpose flour

1 large egg

1 teaspoon baking powder

1 teaspoon smoked paprika

1 teaspoon garlic powder

½ teaspoon freshly ground black pepper

1 cup panko breadcrumbs

1 tablespoon finely chopped fresh dill (optional)

2 large dill pickles, sliced into coins and patted dry with paper towels

Ranch dressing, for serving

1 Fill a medium saucepan with ½ inch of oil. Clip a deep-fry thermometer to the side of the pan and heat the oil over medium-high heat until it reaches 350°F (see Hot Tip, page 79). Line a plate with paper towels.

2 In a medium bowl, whisk together the milk, flour, egg, baking powder, paprika, garlic powder, and pepper until smooth. In a small bowl, combine the panko and dill (if using).

3 When the oil is hot, dip a pickle slice in the batter to coat, letting any excess drip off, then place it in the panko mix and flip to coat both sides. Pop the coated pickle into the hot oil and repeat to coat a few more slices, making sure not to crowd the pan. Cook, adjusting the heat as needed to keep the oil temperature steady, until the pickles are golden brown on the bottom, 2 to 3 minutes. Flip the pickles and cook until golden brown on the second side, 2 to 3 minutes. Use a slotted spoon to transfer the pickle chips to the paper towels to drain. Repeat with the remaining pickle slices, allowing the oil to return to temperature between batches.

4 Serve hot, with ranch dressing alongside for dipping!

To avoid a soggy coating, be mindful of the pickle moisture! Work quickly: DIP each pickle chip into the batter, FLIP it in the panko, and pop it straight into the hot oil to FRY.

FOUR

VEG

Veggie Joes

Growing up, a few meals were in our family's weekly dinner rotation. I think that was my mom's mealtime strategy: Find a recipe that we kids would eat and repeat until we wouldn't (the "keep it simple, stupid" approach). Sloppy joes were one we never seemed to get sick of. I guess the "keep it sloppy, stupid" approach works, too. I can't be sure I would have eaten this veggie-packed version as a kid—actually, I'm certain I wouldn't have, being that mushrooms were my archnemeses. But with age comes a new and deep appreciation for all vegetables, along with a new and deep appreciation for my mom.

Serves 4

1 cup walnuts

8 ounces cremini mushrooms

2 tablespoons extra-virgin olive oil

1 medium yellow onion, diced

2 garlic cloves, minced or grated

3 tablespoons tomato paste

2 tablespoons low-sodium soy sauce

1 teaspoon smoked paprika

1 teaspoon ground cumin

½ teaspoon chili powder

Kosher salt and freshly ground black pepper

⅓ cup ketchup

1 tablespoon light or dark brown sugar

1 tablespoon apple cider vinegar

1 tablespoon Worcestershire sauce (or plant-based Worcestershire, for a vegetarian option)

1 teaspoon Dijon mustard

½ teaspoon garlic powder

4 hamburger buns, or 8 slider buns, toasted (if desired), for serving

Sliced red onion, for serving

Chop Slaw (page 218), for serving (optional)

1 In a food processor, pulse the walnuts a few times to give them a head start, then add the mushrooms and pulse until everything is finely chopped.

2 Heat the olive oil in a large nonstick skillet over medium heat. When the oil is shimmering, add the onion and cook, stirring occasionally, until soft and translucent, about 7 minutes. Add the garlic and cook until fragrant, 1 minute. Add 1 tablespoon of the tomato paste and cook, stirring continuously, until the color has deepened, about 2 minutes. Add the mushroom mixture and cook, stirring occasionally, until the mixture is dry and lightly browned, about 10 minutes. Stir in the soy sauce, paprika, cumin, and chili powder and season with salt and pepper. Cook, stirring and scraping the bottom of the pan, until the flavors meld, 2 to 3 minutes. Taste and adjust the seasoning to your liking.

3 Meanwhile, in a small saucepan, combine ½ cup water, the ketchup, the remaining 2 tablespoons tomato paste, the brown sugar, vinegar, Worcestershire, mustard, and garlic powder. Season with salt and pepper. Bring the mixture to a simmer over medium-low heat. Cook, stirring occasionally, until the sauce thickens slightly, 2 to 3 minutes.

4 Add the sauce to the mushroom and walnut crumble and stir to coat evenly. Bring the mixture to a simmer, stirring occasionally, and cook until heated through. Taste and adjust the seasoning to your liking.

5 Spoon the crumble mixture onto the bottom half of each bun. Top with red onions and slaw, if desired, and finish with the bun tops. Serve immediately!

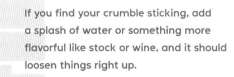

If you find your crumble sticking, add a splash of water or something more flavorful like stock or wine, and it should loosen things right up.

Mushroom al Pastor Tacos

I would have called these Magic Mushroom Tacos because of the extraordinary transformation that takes place here (and the fact that you may forget you're not eating meat), but I was worried that might give you the wrong idea. While this vegetarian take on al pastor won't launch you on a psychedelic trip, these tacos are bursting with savory, smoky goodness that will alter your brain in a different way. No hallucinations—just mouthwatering mushroom magic.

Serves 4

¼ cup pineapple juice

3 tablespoons achiote paste

2 tablespoons fresh lime juice

2 tablespoons fresh orange juice

3 garlic cloves, peeled

1 canned chipotle pepper in adobo, or 1 tablespoon pureed chipotle in adobo

1 teaspoon dried oregano

1 teaspoon ground cumin

1 teaspoon smoked paprika

1 teaspoon kosher salt

½ teaspoon freshly ground black pepper

½ teaspoon ground cinnamon

1 pound cremini mushrooms, sliced

1 small red onion, sliced

1 cup bite-size fresh pineapple chunks

2 tablespoons vegetable oil

For Serving

12 small or 8 medium corn tortillas, warmed

Sour cream

Finely chopped fresh cilantro

Diced white onion

Lime wedges

1   In a blender or food processor, combine the pineapple juice, achiote paste, lime juice, orange juice, garlic, chipotle, oregano, cumin, paprika, salt, pepper, and cinnamon. Blend on medium-high speed until the marinade is smooth and well combined, about 1 minute.

2   In a large bowl, combine the mushrooms, red onion, and pineapple. Pour over the marinade and toss to coat well. Cover the bowl with plastic wrap and marinate in the refrigerator for at least 1 hour or preferably overnight.

3   Position an oven rack about 6 inches from the broiler heat source and preheat the broiler. Line a baking sheet with parchment paper.

4   Use a slotted spoon to transfer the marinated mushroom mixture to the prepared baking sheet (discard the marinade). Drizzle with the oil and toss to combine, then arrange the mixture in a thin, even layer. Broil, flipping a few times to help cook evenly, until the mushrooms are tender, golden brown, and slightly charred on the edges and the onions and pineapple are caramelized, about 20 minutes total (but every broiler is different, so keep an eye on it).

5   Divide the mushroom mixture evenly among the warm tortillas. Top with sour cream, cilantro, onion, and a squeeze of lime juice.

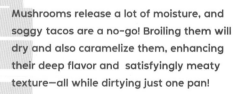

Mushrooms release a lot of moisture, and soggy tacos are a no-go! Broiling them will dry and also caramelize them, enhancing their deep flavor and satisfyingly meaty texture—all while dirtying just one pan!

TIP

Just like a burrito, try not to overstuff the wrappers for easy rolling. Unless you've worked at Chipotle or something, in which case, by all means, overstuff.

Toasted Coconut Tofu Summer Rolls

WITH PEANUT SAUCE

You may have not fallen out of a coconut tree, but these summer rolls sure did. When the weather is hot, the vibes are high, and produce is at its peak, it's time to make these summer rolls. Summer reminds me of popping peanuts at a baseball game, family beach vacations full of piña coladas and sandy cheeks (virgin piñas were my drink of choice as a child), and my dad's garden overflowing with fresh vegetables. This recipe is my best shot at capturing all that nostalgia in a little care package you can eat! Not to mention that summer rolls are the perfect sunny-day food: light, refreshing, and full of fresh veggies. I've dressed up the tender tofu with a crispy toasted coconut coating, but feel free to tailor the fillings and flavors to your own summer memories.

Serves 4

½ cup all-purpose flour

1 teaspoon kosher salt

½ teaspoon freshly ground black pepper

2 large eggs

1 cup unsweetened shredded coconut

1 (14-ounce) block firm tofu, drained and pressed (see Hot Tip, page 133)

½ cup any creamy peanut butter

3 tablespoons low-sodium soy sauce

2 tablespoons honey

1 tablespoon rice vinegar

1 garlic clove, minced

½ teaspoon grated fresh ginger

½ teaspoon toasted sesame oil

Juice of ½ lime, plus more if needed

¼ cup warm water

8 rice paper wrappers

¼ small head of green or purple cabbage, very thinly sliced

2 medium carrots, cut into thin matchsticks

½ English cucumber, or 1 to 2 Persian cucumbers, cut into thin matchsticks

½ cup fresh mint leaves

½ cup fresh cilantro

3 scallions, cut into thirds crosswise, then sliced lengthwise

1 jalapeño, seeded and cut into matchsticks

1 Preheat the oven to 375°F. Line a baking sheet with parchment paper.

2 In a shallow dish, stir together the flour, half the salt, and half the pepper. Beat the eggs in a separate shallow dish. Spread the coconut evenly over a third shallow dish and season with the remaining salt and pepper.

3 Cut the tofu crosswise into 8 rectangles, then halve each rectangle lengthwise so you have 16 long, skinny pieces. Dip one tofu slice into the flour mixture, shaking off any excess, then into the egg, allowing any excess to drip off. Dredge the tofu in the coconut, pressing it to coat all sides, then place on the prepared pan. Repeat with the remaining tofu.

4 Bake the tofu for 20 to 25 minutes, flipping halfway through, until the coconut is golden and toasted.

5 Meanwhile, in a small bowl, whisk together the peanut butter, soy sauce, honey, vinegar, garlic, ginger, sesame oil, and lime juice. While whisking, gradually add the warm water until the sauce reaches your desired consistency. Taste and adjust the seasoning to your liking.

6 Fill a wide, shallow dish with warm water. Place one rice paper wrapper in the water and soak until it just begins to soften, 10 to 15 seconds. Place the softened wrapper on a clean, dry surface. Lay 2 pieces of the coconut-crusted tofu on the lower third of the wrapper. Top with cabbage, carrots, cucumber, mint, cilantro, scallions, and jalapeño, or any combination as desired! Fold the sides of the wrapper over the filling, then gently roll up the wrapper from the bottom, tucking the filling tightly as you go. Place the summer roll on a serving platter and repeat with the remaining ingredients.

7 Serve the summer rolls with the peanut sauce alongside for dipping.

Creamy Goat Cheese Orzetto
WITH CHERRY TOMATO CHECCA

Orzo may be the little guy in the pasta world, but as someone who is 5 foot 3, I'm here to tell you never to underestimate the little guy (or girl). Alongside creamy goat cheese, which brings a unique zest and funk, we have a fresh tomato checca, basically an uncooked tomato sauce. This orzo dish proves size doesn't matter when it comes to taste, because while it may be petite, the flavors are anything but.

Serves 4

Checca

1 cup quartered cherry tomatoes

2 tablespoons extra-virgin olive oil

2 tablespoons torn fresh basil leaves, plus more for serving

2 garlic cloves, minced or grated

Kosher salt and freshly ground black pepper

Orzo

3 very ripe medium tomatoes

1 tablespoon extra-virgin olive oil

1 medium yellow onion, diced

2 garlic cloves, minced or grated

1½ cups orzo

2 tablespoons tomato paste

Kosher salt

¼ teaspoon red pepper flakes

½ cup dry white wine (I like sauvignon blanc)

Freshly ground black pepper

2 cups low-sodium vegetable stock

2 to 3 ounces creamy goat cheese

¼ cup freshly grated Parmigiano Reggiano cheese, plus more for serving

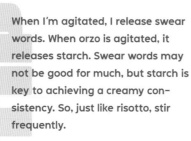

When I'm agitated, I release swear words. When orzo is agitated, it releases starch. Swear words may not be good for much, but starch is key to achieving a creamy consistency. So, just like risotto, stir frequently.

1 Make the checca. In a small bowl, combine the cherry tomatoes, olive oil, basil, and garlic. Taste and season with salt and black pepper to your liking. Set aside to marinate while you prepare the rest of the dish.

2 Make the orzo. Grate the tomatoes on the medium holes of a box grater set over a medium bowl until all that's left in your hand is the skin; discard the skins.

3 Heat the olive oil in a large skillet over medium-low heat. When the oil is shimmering, add the onion and cook, stirring occasionally, until soft and translucent, about 10 minutes. Add the garlic and cook until fragrant, 1 minute. Stir in the orzo. Cook, stirring continuously, to toast the orzo, about 2 minutes. Add the tomato paste and cook, stirring continuously, until the orzo is golden, 2 minutes more, adjusting the heat as needed to prevent scorching. Season with a big pinch of salt and the red pepper flakes.

4 Pour in the wine and cook, stirring continuously, until the alcohol has cooked off (you should be able to smell the difference), about 4 minutes. Stir in the grated tomatoes and season with salt and black pepper.

5 Reduce the heat to low. Add ½ cup of the stock and cook, stirring continuously, until the orzo has absorbed all the liquid; continue adding the stock ½ cup at a time and waiting until it has been absorbed before adding more. Cook until the mixture is soft but still has some bite, 10 to 15 minutes. Taste and season with more salt and black pepper to your liking.

6 Add the goat cheese to taste and stir until it melts and creates a creamy sauce. Stir in the Parm. Taste and adjust the seasoning one last time. Cook, stirring often, until the sauce thickens and coats the tomatoes and orzo, 2 to 3 minutes more.

7 Transfer the orzo to a serving dish and top with dollops of the checca, then sprinkle with more Parm and basil. Serve hot and enjoy!

Almond-Crusted Eggplant Parm

Listen, I'm not going to sugarcoat it, or in this case, almond-coat it. This recipe isn't going to take the place of chicken Parm. I'm not one of those people who pretends zucchini tastes like pasta. But for the sake of those who don't eat meat, or for those days when we meat eaters want something else, this is a satisfying vegetarian option. The eggplant is sturdy enough to hold up in cooking, the almond coating gives the dish a nutty twist, and truthfully, I'd eat anything doused in marinara sauce and bubbling mozzarella.

Serves 4

Extra-virgin olive oil, for greasing and drizzling

1 large eggplant, sliced into ½-inch-thick rounds

Kosher salt

1 cup almond meal

½ cup freshly grated Parmigiano Reggiano cheese, plus more for serving

1 teaspoon dried basil

1 teaspoon dried oregano

Freshly ground black pepper

1 cup all-purpose flour (or almond flour, for a gluten-free option)

2 large eggs

2 cups marinara sauce

1 (12-ounce) log fresh mozzarella cheese, sliced

Torn fresh basil leaves, for serving

They say for a long life, you should sweat every day. Well, sweating reduces bitterness, in both humans and eggplants.

1   Preheat the oven to 375°F. Grease a baking sheet with olive oil.

2   Place the eggplant slices on a clean kitchen towel or paper towels and generously sprinkle with salt. Let stand at room temperature for about 30 minutes to draw out moisture. Pat the eggplant slices dry with paper towels, pressing gently to remove any remaining moisture.

3   In a shallow dish, combine the almond meal, Parm, basil, and oregano and season with salt and pepper. Taste the almond mixture and adjust the seasoning to your liking. Place the flour in a separate shallow dish. Beat the eggs in a third shallow dish.

4   Working with one at a time, dredge an eggplant slice in the flour, shaking off any excess, then dip it into the egg, ensuring it's coated on both sides and allowing any excess to drip off (see Hot Tip, page 165). Dredge the eggplant slice in the almond meal mixture, pressing to adhere evenly on both sides. Transfer the coated slice to the prepared baking sheet and repeat with the remaining eggplant. Drizzle the tops of the coated eggplant slices with olive oil.

5   Bake for 20 to 25 minutes, flipping the slices halfway through, until the eggplant is tender and the crust is lightly golden and crispy. Remove from the oven (keep the oven on).

6   Spread a thin layer of marinara sauce over the bottom of a 9×13-inch baking dish. Arrange the baked eggplant slices on top of the marinara, slightly overlapping and shingling them to create a single layer. Pour the remaining marinara over the eggplant slices. Place the mozzarella slices on top of the eggplant, covering them generously.

7   Bake the eggplant Parmesan for 15 to 20 minutes, until the cheese is melted and bubbling. (For a golden and slightly crispy topping, switch the oven to broil and cook for 1 to 2 minutes, until the cheese on top is lightly browned.) Garnish with basil and more Parm and serve hot.

Zoya's Lasagna

Credit where credit's due: This is not my recipe—it's Zoya's. But what's hers is mine, right? When I asked her if I could "borrow" her lasagna recipe for my cookbook (because it's *that* good), she graciously agreed, meaning she said, "Fine, but I better get a shout-out." So I said hold my fork and gave her the title. I can't be sure Zoya will ever write a cookbook, so it's my duty as a doting partner to ensure this recipe is published. Zoya and I are the official cooks of our friend group, and this is what they all request. It's like a classic vegetarian lasagna, but made better with Zoya's Persian touch.

Serves 8 to 10

½ cup (1 stick) unsalted butter, plus more if needed

2 tablespoons extra-virgin olive oil, plus more if needed

1 large yellow onion, diced

8 garlic cloves, minced or grated

2 teaspoons kosher salt, plus more as needed

2 teaspoons freshly ground black pepper

1 teaspoon sweet paprika

1 teaspoon ground turmeric

1 teaspoon ground cumin

1 teaspoon red pepper flakes

4 hot Italian Beyond sausages or veggie sausages of choice, thawed, if frozen

¼ cup tomato paste

¼ cup white wine (Zoya likes sauvignon blanc or pinot grigio) or water

Juice of ½ lemon

2 (28-ounce) cans whole peeled tomatoes (preferably San Marzano), with their juices

½ cup fresh basil leaves, finely chopped, plus more for serving

2 (15-ounce) containers whole-milk ricotta cheese

Zest of 1 lemon

2 (12-ounce) packages oven-ready lasagna noodles

1 (16-ounce) bag shredded mozzarella cheese

1 cup freshly grated Parmigiano Reggiano cheese, plus more for serving

1 (8-ounce) ball fresh mozzarella cheese, sliced, or additional shredded mozzarella

Nonstick cooking spray

1 Preheat the oven to 350°F. Grease a deep 9×13-inch baking dish with butter or olive oil.

2 Heat the butter and oil in a large saucepan over medium heat. When the butter has melted, add the onion and garlic and cook, stirring occasionally, until soft and translucent, about 7 minutes. Season with the salt, black pepper, paprika, turmeric, cumin, and red pepper flakes and stir to coat. Move the onion to the edges of the pan, making space in the center. Add the veggie sausage and cook, breaking it up with a wooden spoon, until lightly browned, about 7 minutes. Add the tomato paste and cook, stirring continuously, until the color has deepened, 2 to 3 minutes more, then stir to incorporate all the ingredients in the pan.

3 Add the wine and half the lemon juice. Cook, stirring often, until the alcohol cooks off (you should be able to smell the difference), about 2 minutes. Add the tomatoes with their juices and break them down with your spoon into very small pieces. (This takes some work, but it's worth it!) Remove from the heat and stir in the basil. Taste and adjust the seasoning to your liking.

4 In a medium bowl, stir together the ricotta, lemon zest, and remaining lemon juice to combine. Taste and season with salt and black pepper to your liking.

5 Pour a thin layer of tomato sauce over the bottom of the prepared baking dish. Add 1 layer of lasagna noodles, trying not to overlap them (break the noodles as needed to fit). Add a layer of 1 cup of the sauce, then ½ cup of the ricotta mixture, then a heaping ½ cup of the shredded mozzarella, and then sprinkle with 2 tablespoons of the Parm. Repeat with the remaining ingredients six more times, making eight noodle layers total and stacking the ingredients until you reach the top of the pan. For the final layer, add the remaining sauce and top with the remaining Parm and the fresh mozzarella

**Lasagna pans are foiled so your
lasagna plans won't be.**

(if using; if not, top with more shredded mozzarella). Pour 1 tablespoon water into each corner of the baking dish to prevent the lasagna from drying out. Spray a sheet of aluminum foil with cooking spray, then cover the pan tightly with the foil, sprayed-side down. Place the baking dish on a baking sheet.

6   Bake for 30 to 40 minutes, until the cheese has melted and the sauce is bubbling. Remove the foil and switch the oven to broil. Cook for a few minutes more, until the cheese is browned—careful, as this happens fast! Remove from the oven and let the lasagna sit for 15 to 20 minutes. Top with more fresh basil and Parm before serving.

Lentil Shepherd's Pie

Shepherd's pie dates back to the 1700s, making it a long-standing favorite, especially among "meat and potatoes" people. Three centuries later, I think it's time for a plant-powered makeover—but don't worry, you can still have your pie and eat it, too. This shepherd's pie is reimagined with a base of aromatics and lentils stewed in a complex sauce flavored with tomato paste, soy sauce, and plant-based Worcestershire to add depth and character (or the regular kind if you're not veg!). Topped with fluffy clouds of mashed potatoes, it's both a nod to tradition and a bold step into the future of veggies as mains. This is a pie that has truly come full circle.

Serves 6

2 tablespoons extra-virgin olive oil

1 large yellow onion, diced

2 medium carrots, diced

2 celery stalks, diced

3 garlic cloves, minced or grated

2 tablespoons tomato paste

2 tablespoons low-sodium soy sauce

2 tablespoons plant-based Worcestershire sauce (I like Wa Jan Shan brand)

1 teaspoon dried thyme

1 teaspoon dried rosemary

1 teaspoon smoked paprika

1 cup dried green or brown lentils, rinsed and drained

4 cups low-sodium vegetable stock or water

Kosher salt and freshly ground black pepper

½ cup frozen peas

½ cup frozen corn kernels

2 pounds potatoes, such as russets or Yukon Golds, peeled and cut into chunks

½ cup heavy cream

4 tablespoons (½ stick) unsalted butter

1 cup freshly grated Parmigiano Reggiano cheese, plus more for serving

2 large egg yolks

Finely chopped fresh parsley or chives, for serving

1 Preheat the oven to 375°F.

2 Heat the olive oil in a large cast-iron or other ovenproof skillet over medium heat. When the oil is shimmering, add the onion, carrots, and celery. Cook, stirring occasionally, until the vegetables soften, about 7 minutes. Stir in the garlic and cook until fragrant, 1 minute. Add the tomato paste, soy sauce, Worcestershire, thyme, rosemary, and paprika. Stir to coat. Add the lentils and cook, stirring often, until the color and flavor of the tomato paste have deepened, 2 to 3 minutes.

3 Pour in the stock and bring the mixture to a simmer. Cover and cook, stirring occasionally, until the lentils are al dente and beginning to soften and some of the liquid has been absorbed, 12 to 15 minutes. Season with salt and pepper. Stir in the peas and corn and simmer until everything is heated through and tender, 2 to 3 minutes. Taste and adjust the seasoning to your liking.

4 Meanwhile, place the potatoes in a large pot and add water to cover. Salt the water so it's salty like the tears of happiness you will cry when you taste this pie. Bring the water to a boil over medium-high heat, then cook until the potato chunks are tender, about 12 minutes (timing will vary depending on the size of the chunks, so check often).

5 Meanwhile, combine the cream and butter in a small saucepan and heat over medium heat until steaming.

6 Drain the potatoes and return them to the pot. Add the butter mixture, ½ cup of the Parm, and the egg yolks. Using a handheld mixer on low speed or a potato masher, mash the potatoes until smooth and creamy. Taste and season with salt and pepper to your liking.

7 Dollop the mashed potato topping over the lentil filling in the skillet, then carefully spread it out, covering the lentils

The main culprits for gluey mash are overcooking and overmashing. Starting them in cold water helps them cook more evenly, getting them to fork-tender (but not mushy). Drain well, and remember not to overmash. Keep it light and fluffy, not sticky and clumpy!

entirely without mixing the two together. Use a fork to create some designs in the surface of the mashed potatoes, if you like. Sprinkle the remaining ½ cup Parm over the top.

8   Bake the shepherd's pie for 25 to 30 minutes, until the top is golden and the filling is bubbling. (If the top isn't as golden as you like, switch on the broiler and cook for a few minutes more, watching it carefully to prevent burning.) Remove from the oven and let cool slightly before serving.

9   Serve topped with more Parm and some parsley.

Butter Butter Beans

We're giving one of my all-time favorite Indian classics, butter chicken, a delightful vegetarian twist. Call them double butter beans or even butter² beans—whatever you choose, they're sure to make you bean with joy! These buttery beans are nestled in a dreamy and creamy tomato sauce that's spiced to perfection. Serve them as a satisfying side dish with rice or enjoy them as a main course alongside naan or crusty bread.

Serves 4

2 tablespoons unsalted butter or ghee

1 large yellow onion, finely diced

3 garlic cloves, minced or grated

1 (1-inch) piece fresh ginger, peeled and minced

1 teaspoon ground cumin

1 teaspoon ground coriander

1 teaspoon ground turmeric

1 teaspoon garam masala, plus more to taste

½ teaspoon cayenne pepper, plus more to taste

Kosher salt and freshly ground black pepper

2 tablespoons tomato paste

1 (15-ounce) can diced tomatoes

1 cup heavy cream, plus more as needed

2 (15-ounce) cans butter beans, drained and rinsed

Fresh cilantro, for serving

1   Melt the butter in a large skillet or saucepan over medium heat. Add the onion and cook, stirring occasionally, until translucent and beginning to brown, about 10 minutes. Add the garlic and ginger and cook until fragrant, another minute or so. Stir in the cumin, coriander, turmeric, garam masala, and cayenne. Cook, stirring often, until toasted and fragrant, a minute or two. Season with salt and black pepper.

2   Move the onion to the edges of the pan, making space in the center. Add the tomato paste to the skillet and cook, stirring continuously, until the color (and flavors!) deepen, 2 to 3 minutes, then stir to incorporate all the ingredients in the pan. Pour in the diced tomatoes with their juices. Simmer, stirring occasionally, until the flavors have melded, 5 to 7 minutes. Pour in the cream, stir, and simmer until a rich, creamy sauce forms, about 5 minutes. Season with salt and black pepper again.

3   Gently fold in the butter beans, being sure they are well coated in the sauce. Simmer until the beans are heated through, 5 to 7 minutes. If the sauce is too thick, add a splash of water or more cream to achieve your desired consistency.

4   Taste and season one last time with salt and black pepper to your liking. Adjust the other spices to your preference, adding more cayenne for heat or more garam masala for depth of flavor. When the beans are heated through and the flavors are well balanced, remove the skillet from the heat. Serve hot, garnished with cilantro.

HOT TIP
Let's have a toast for tomato paste. Actually, though, you need to toast it to taste it. Frying tomato paste in a little bit of fat helps get rid of its metallic taste and caramelizes its sugars, deepening its flavor.

Sesame-Soy Glazed Tofu Bowls

I am not a vegetarian myself, but having a dedicated space for non-meat eaters in this cookbook was important to me. While I might never put down my steak knife for good, I wholeheartedly believe in balance and an open mind—plus, incorporating vegetarian and vegan meals into my repertoire genuinely brings me joy. Contrary to popular belief, meat eaters can love tofu, too. Tofu is all about preparation: It absorbs flavor like a sponge, so if your tofu is bland, don't blame the tofu—blame yourself (and then forgive yourself). These bowls are quick and easy to prepare, perfect for a busy weeknight dinner, and just might make you fall in love with tofu.

Serves 4

⅓ cup low-sodium soy sauce

¼ cup rice vinegar

¼ cup honey or maple syrup

2 tablespoons toasted sesame oil

2 tablespoons minced fresh ginger

4 garlic cloves, minced or grated

1 (14-ounce) block firm tofu, drained, pressed (see Hot Tip), and cut into 1-inch cubes

2 tablespoons vegetable oil

1 tablespoon cornstarch

2 tablespoons sesame seeds

For Serving

2 cups cooked short-grain rice

Sliced English or Persian cucumber

Sliced avocado

Shelled edamame

Sliced scallions

Sesame seeds

Fresh cilantro

Chile oil (a must!)

1   In a medium bowl, whisk together the soy sauce, vinegar, honey, sesame oil, ginger, and garlic until smooth. Add the tofu and toss gently to coat. Set the tofu aside to marinate at room temperature for at least 20 minutes, or cover and refrigerate overnight, stirring once or twice.

2   Heat the vegetable oil in a large nonstick skillet over medium-high heat. When the oil is shimmering, remove the tofu from the bowl, shaking off any excess marinade, and place it in the hot skillet—reserve the remaining marinade. Cook the tofu, stirring and flipping occasionally, until golden and crispy, 7 to 8 minutes total. Remove the pan from the heat.

3   Whisk the cornstarch into the reserved marinade until no lumps remain. Add the marinade and sesame seeds to the pan and cook over medium heat, stirring continuously, until the sauce is bubbling and thickened and coats the tofu, 1 to 2 minutes.

4   Place a serving of cooked rice in the bottom of four bowls. Arrange cucumber, avocado, and edamame around the rice in each bowl. Top the bowls with the crispy glazed tofu, dividing it evenly. Garnish with scallions, sesame seeds, and cilantro. Drizzle with chile oil and enjoy!

HOW TO PRESS TOFU FOR DUMMIES (I would know, I'm a dummy): Plate → paper towels → tofu → paper towels → heavy pan → sit for 30 minutes to 1 hour. See how easy that was?

Sunshine Stew

When winter's gloom casts its chilly shadow, we all yearn for a touch of sunshine. Zoya is one of those people who needs an extra ray of light during those darker days. That's how this recipe was born. It's a heartwarming concoction of golden-yellow split peas, warming turmeric, and comforting potatoes, like a homemade bowl of sunshine when the real thing is scarce. Just as the sun breaks through the clouds, this stew bursts with flavor and warmth, offering a nourishing hug for the soul. So ladle up a bowl and let the sun-kissed goodness fill your heart. I hope it brightens even your dreariest days.

Serves 4

2 tablespoons vegetable oil

1 large yellow onion, diced

2 garlic cloves, minced or grated

1 teaspoon ground turmeric

Kosher salt and freshly ground black pepper

2 tablespoons tomato paste

2 medium yellow potatoes, peeled or unpeeled (up to you!) and chopped

4 cups low-sodium vegetable stock

1 cup dried yellow split peas or red lentils, soaked, drained, and rinsed

Juice of ½ lemon

For Serving

Labneh or plain full-fat Greek yogurt

Finely chopped fresh parsley

Freshly grated Parmigiano Reggiano cheese

1 lemon

1   Heat the vegetable oil in a large pot over medium heat. When the oil is shimmering, add the onion and cook, stirring occasionally, until soft and translucent, about 7 minutes. Add the garlic and cook until fragrant, another minute. Add the turmeric and season with salt and pepper. Add the tomato paste and cook, stirring often, until the color deepens, 2 to 3 minutes.

2   Add the potatoes to the pot and cook, stirring often, until they begin to soften, about 3 minutes. Pour in the stock and split peas. Increase the heat to high and bring to a boil, then reduce the heat to low, cover, and simmer, stirring occasionally to avoid sticking, until the split peas and potatoes are tender, 25 to 30 minutes.

3   Stir in the lemon juice, then season with salt and pepper. Taste and adjust the seasoning to your liking. Simmer, uncovered, for 5 to 10 minutes more to allow the flavors to meld.

4   Ladle the stew into bowls and top each with a spoonful of labneh. Sprinkle with parsley and Parm and grate a little zest from the lemon on top of each. Cut the lemon into wedges and serve the stew hot, with the lemon wedges on the side!

We want sun*shine* not sun*burnt.* Remember to reduce the heat to low after the boil and stir frequently. If you do scorch the bottom, do not scrape the burned part into your stew! Transfer the good stuff into a clean pot and leave the blackened bits behind.

Three-Bean Chili Cornbread Potpie

I'm a big bean lover—call me a beanie baby. This recipe has THREE kinds; the more beans the merrier, right? Chili is the quintessential comfort meal, perfect for a cozy night in or to share with family and friends. And a rich, hearty chili topped with a toasty blanket of cornbread? Even better.

Serves 6 to 8

Chili

1 tablespoon extra-virgin olive oil

1 large yellow or red onion, diced

1 red bell pepper, diced

1 green bell pepper, diced

1 jalapeño, seeded, if desired, and finely chopped

2 garlic cloves, minced or grated

1 tablespoon chili powder

1 tablespoon ground cumin

1 tablespoon sweet paprika

1 teaspoon dried oregano

1 (28-ounce) can diced tomatoes, with their juices

2 cups low-sodium vegetable stock

1 (15-ounce) can black beans, drained and rinsed

1 (15-ounce) can kidney beans, drained and rinsed

1 (15-ounce) can pinto beans, drained and rinsed

Kosher salt and freshly ground black pepper

Cornbread

1 cup medium-grind cornmeal

1 cup all-purpose flour

⅓ cup freshly grated cheddar cheese

⅓ cup sliced scallions

¼ cup sugar

1 tablespoon baking powder

½ teaspoon kosher salt

1 cup buttermilk, at room temperature

4 tablespoons (½ stick) unsalted butter, melted and cooled

1 large egg, at room temperature

Toppings (choose one or many)

Shredded cheese

Sour cream

Sliced scallions

Finely chopped fresh cilantro

Or any other favorites!

1   Make the chili. Heat the olive oil in a large pot or Dutch oven over medium heat. When the oil is shimmering, add the onion, bell peppers, jalapeño, and garlic. Cook, stirring often, until softened, about 7 minutes. Add the chili powder, cumin, paprika, and oregano. Stir well to coat the vegetables in the spices and toast them a bit. Pour in the diced tomatoes with their juices and the stock. Gently stir in all the beans. Season with salt and black pepper.

2   Bring the chili to a simmer, then reduce the heat to low, cover, and cook, stirring occasionally, until it thickens, 20 to 30 minutes. Taste and adjust the seasoning to your liking.

3   Meanwhile, make the cornbread. Preheat the oven to 425°F.

4   In a large bowl, combine the cornmeal, flour, cheddar, scallions, sugar, baking powder, and salt. In a medium bowl, whisk together the buttermilk, melted butter, and egg until the mixture is smooth. Pour the wet ingredients into the dry and stir until just combined. Do not overmix (see Hot Tip)!

5   If your pot isn't ovenproof, transfer the chili to a baking dish. Dollop the cornbread batter evenly over the chili and gently spread it into an even layer—do not stir. Bake for 15 to 30 minutes, until the cornbread is golden brown and a toothpick inserted into the center comes out clean.

6   Let cool for 5 to 10 minutes, then serve the cornbread and chili hot, with the toppings of your choice.

Don't lose those lovely little lumps! Your cornbread batter should be lumpy when you bake it. If you're mixing it until it's smooth, you're likely *over*mixing, which will result in dense cornbread.

TASTY DAYS AND SLEEPLESS NIGHTS

What Tasty gave me went far beyond a paycheck: Tasty gave me a chance.

They say luck is when preparation meets opportunity. I've always felt lucky—opportunity strikes all the time—but it's always up to me to be ready to jump. After college, I didn't see a place for me in the kitchen, so I dove in wherever I could and learned. I found myself in Stockholm cooking for a family, working as a food stylist on my hours off, prepping avocados in the back of a taco truck on weekends, and posting pictures and blurbs on my food blog at night. I wasn't sure what I was working toward, but I kept going. A year later, a door appeared: a listing for an internship at Tasty, a new but already monstrous digital food network.

I remember the first time I saw a Tasty video. Lying in bed scrolling Facebook, when hands making some combination of cheese, bacon, and bread flashed across my screen. I remember thinking I could do that. Not in a snarky way, but in a "this is my golden ticket!" way. I applied for the internship while in Sweden and held all my interviews via Skype at odd hours of the night. When they asked me what my video experience was, I told them, "Tell me what button to push, and I'll push it." My boldness made up for my lack of experience, and they decided to take a chance on me.

I had one week to move from Sweden to LA. The Tasty team consisted mostly of video people who had learned food. I was a food person who had to learn video. I promised myself I would put my head down and learn as much as I possibly could, mostly to secure a job that I wanted desperately. We spent the first month in a film school crash course. Interns weren't allowed to make videos until after the course, but I was eager to get started. I shadowed the producers, washing their dishes, doing their grocery shopping, taking video, audio, editing, and lighting classes, all the while dreaming of the day I would be at my very own shooting table.

I decided my first video would be a banana pull apart bread. Monkey bread was going viral online; the flavor was a play on banana bread, a personal favorite. It had all the makings of a viral video, or so I thought. The rush of watching my first video go live is a feeling I still chase. After it went up, I texted my mentor, Alvin, "It's live! How is it doing?" I didn't yet understand video metrics. "Good, but not viral," he replied. Good wasn't enough for me: I wanted viral.

Tasty became my life. I was churning out videos and exceeding my quota. My managers told me to slow down, that I would burn out; I had never heard that term before. People have always called me an Energizer bunny. The bunny doesn't burn out. My second video did better, but still not viral. I felt like I was trying to crack the Da Vinci Code. In one of our weekly brainstorms, it hit me. I can't just replicate virality, I need to be virality. From then on, I spent less time online and more time in my imagination, daydreaming of my next big hit.

"What if I made lasagna, but with chicken? Pieces of pounded-out chicken instead of lasagna noodles, chicken parm meets lasagna." The odd looks I got after throwing out that idea is my Roman Empire. The consensus was that it was too weird. But I thought the flavors fit too well together, like a puzzle. That's what a viral recipe is to me: a puzzle with endless combinations. Despite everyone's judgment, I moved forward. At the next week's brainstorm, we were all discussing the success of my first viral video, Chicken Parm Lasagna.

Virality doesn't necessarily mean everyone likes it. Rather, it means it evokes emotions that connect us as human beings. It felt like the floodgates had opened, and my next three videos each hit a million shares. I had hit my stride; my lack of any real culinary training served me well there, as I was catering to home cooks like me. I felt like I would be at Tasty forever.

My job was to be behind the camera, a pair of hands cooking. When Tasty launched a YouTube channel, there was some hesitation to put me in front of the camera, but I was itching for a new challenge. Ultimately, the team knew my silly nature could work online, so we started with Behind Tasty.

In the first behind-the-scenes video, a rainbow crepe cake, I was just the camera operator. It didn't feel like an accurate representation of my job. For the next Behind Tasty, I asked if I could show my actual job, filming AND cooking. I wanted a challenge, so I settled on making chocolate croissants. I showed up as my goofy, clumsy self, and my Behind Tasty videos were an instant hit. We were just having fun; I never anticipated millions of people would tune in and feel inspired to cook because they saw someone making mistakes in the kitchen for the first time. We showed the process of trial and error, how I learned along the way without giving up, and course-correcting until each dish came out just right, or at least close enough.

I thought producing Tasty videos was my endgame, but the lightbulb turned on when I got to be on camera. It felt like everything I had done prior, all the preparation met with each opportunity, had finally caught up with the most significant opportunity of all. Whether it was luck or fate, I had finally aligned with my purpose.

FIVE

CHICKEN

Harissa & Yogurt–Marinated Chicken Tacos

It's no wonder this recipe lands on page 143—this was the first thing I ever cooked for Zoya. You could say it sealed the deal, but that would be a lie, because she took several more months to come around to dating me. She did say these were some of the best tacos she'd ever had, so they probably helped. BUT I DIGRESS. I'm a wimp with spicy food, but Zoya loves it, so I figured out a way to make us both happy. This taco is the perfect pair, just like us: You have the fiery chile harissa to heat things up, and the cooling yogurt to mellow everything out. Plus, the creamy, herby, zesty dressing on the slaw is sure to make sparks fly.

Serves 4

Chicken

1 to 1¼ pounds boneless, skinless chicken thighs

1 cup plain full-fat Greek yogurt

¼ cup harissa

Juice of ½ lime

1 (1-inch) piece fresh ginger, peeled and grated

2 garlic cloves, minced or grated

½ teaspoon ground cumin

½ teaspoon red pepper flakes

½ teaspoon kosher salt

Vegetable oil, for greasing

Cilantro-Lime Slaw

1 cup plain full-fat Greek yogurt

½ cup packed fresh cilantro

Juice of ½ lime

1 garlic clove, peeled

1 teaspoon honey (optional)

½ teaspoon ground cumin

Kosher salt and freshly ground black pepper

2 cups chopped green or purple cabbage or bagged coleslaw mix

For Serving

8 small tortillas (I like blended corn and wheat tortillas), warmed

Harissa

Pickled onions

Sliced radishes

Finely chopped fresh cilantro

Lime wedges

1 Make the chicken. Place the chicken in a 9-inch square baking dish. In a small bowl, stir together the yogurt, harissa, lime juice, ginger, garlic, cumin, red pepper flakes, and salt until smooth. Pour the marinade over the chicken and flip the chicken to coat. Cover with plastic wrap and marinate in the fridge for at least 2 hours or up to 24 hours.

2 Heat a large cast-iron skillet over medium heat and brush it with a little bit of oil. When the pan is hot, remove the chicken from the marinade, allowing the excess to drip off, and place it in the skillet. Cook until brown and crispy, about 5 minutes. Flip and cook until the chicken is cooked through (an instant-read thermometer should register 165°F), 5 minutes or so more. Remove the chicken from the pan and let it rest for 5 minutes, then shred it.

3 Meanwhile, make the slaw. In a blender or food processor, combine the yogurt, cilantro, lime juice, garlic, honey (if using), and cumin and season with salt and black pepper. Blend on medium-high speed until smooth, about 1 minute. Taste and adjust the seasoning to your liking.

4 In a medium bowl, combine the cabbage and ⅓ cup of the dressing and mix until the cabbage is well coated. Taste and add more dressing, if you like. (Any remaining dressing can be refrigerated for up to 3 days.)

5 Spread each tortilla with harissa, then divide the chicken and slaw among them. Set out the rest of the toppings for DIY tacos!

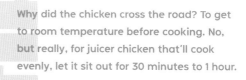

Why did the chicken cross the road? To get to room temperature before cooking. No, but really, for juicer chicken that'll cook evenly, let it sit out for 30 minutes to 1 hour.

Mustardy Chicken & Mustard Greens

I love chicken with a classic pan sauce. And no, pan sauce is not just sauce made in a pan—it's a flavorful liquid created by deglazing the pan you've used to sear something. Here we use liquid—stock and wine—to lift the flavorful browned bits the chicken left stuck to the bottom of the pan (it's called "fond," if you want to be fancy). The bits dissolve into the liquid, creating a ridiculously flavorful base for your dinner. For our last trick, we add a few other ingredients, including two kinds of mustard, to make a deliciously rich sauce. I like to throw in some greens to hit my quota for the day. This dish is classic and elegant—much like a good mustard, it really knows how to spice things up.

Serves 4 to 6

2 pounds boneless, skinless chicken thighs or breasts

Kosher salt and freshly ground black pepper

4 tablespoons (½ stick) unsalted butter

2 tablespoons extra-virgin olive oil

1 medium yellow onion, diced

2 garlic cloves, minced or grated

1 cup low-sodium chicken stock

½ cup dry white wine (I like sauvignon blanc)

2 tablespoons Dijon mustard

1 tablespoon whole-grain mustard

½ cup heavy cream

1 bunch mustard greens or collards, leaves stemmed and thinly sliced

Juice of ½ lemon

Finely chopped fresh parsley, for serving

1   Season the chicken generously with salt and pepper on both sides. In a large skillet, heat the butter with the olive oil over medium-high heat. When the butter has melted, add the chicken and cook, tilting the pan and spooning the butter and oil over the chicken as it cooks, until golden brown and cooked through (it should register 165°F on an instant-read thermometer), 4 to 5 minutes per side. Transfer the chicken to a plate and tent it with aluminum foil to keep warm.

2   Add the onion to the skillet and cook, stirring often, until soft and translucent, about 3 minutes. Add the garlic and cook until fragrant, 1 minute. Pour in the stock and wine and cook, scraping up any browned bits from the bottom of the skillet and adjusting the heat to ensure the liquid doesn't boil, until the wine is simmering and the bottom of the pan is mostly clean, just a few seconds. Stir in both mustards. Return to a simmer, then reduce the heat to medium-low and stir in the cream. Simmer the sauce until it thickens slightly, 2 to 3 minutes. Stir in the greens and cook until wilted, about 4 minutes.

3   Return the chicken to the skillet along with any juices on the plate and spoon some of the pan sauce over the top. Simmer for 5 minutes, until the flavors have melded. Stir in the lemon juice. Taste and adjust the seasoning.

4   To serve, transfer the greens to a serving platter. Arrange the chicken on top and spoon the mustard pan sauce over the chicken. Sprinkle with parsley and enjoy!

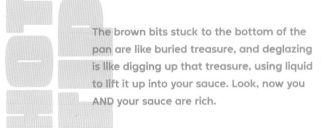

The brown bits stuck to the bottom of the pan are like buried treasure, and deglazing is like digging up that treasure, using liquid to lift it up into your sauce. Look, now you AND your sauce are rich.

Artichoke Chicken Piccata

Fancy but not fussy, simple but not boring, chicken piccata is one of my all-time favorite weeknight meals, and I knew I wanted to share a recipe with you. (It's so nice I ended up doing it twice—I couldn't help myself! See the Scallops Piccata on page 173.) I also knew you probably already have a classic go-to piccata recipe. While thinking about how to spice things up (not literally) and what would pair well with the briny and acidic flavors of the dish, I thought artichokes just might do the trick. I threw in some dill because, as you might have gathered by now, it's my favorite herb. And now this chokey piccata has me in a chokehold.

Serves 4

4 boneless, skinless chicken breasts (6 to 8 ounces each)

2 teaspoons kosher salt, plus more as needed

½ teaspoon freshly ground black pepper

4 tablespoons extra-virgin olive oil

½ cup all-purpose flour

2 tablespoons unsalted butter

4 garlic cloves, minced or grated

½ cup dry white wine (I like sauvignon blanc)

½ cup low-sodium chicken stock

Zest and juice of 1 lemon

1 (14-ounce) can artichoke hearts packed in water, drained and halved

1 tablespoon finely chopped fresh dill, plus more for serving

¼ cup heavy cream

3 tablespoons drained capers

1 lemon, cut into wedges

Cooked spaghetti or angel hair pasta, for serving (optional)

Not to sound crass, but you need to take your chicken breasts to pound town. Pounding the chicken both tenderizes the meat and promotes even cooking.

1   Place one chicken breast on your cutting board and use a very sharp knife to slice through the center horizontally, holding your knife parallel to the cutting board and stopping about ½ inch from the other side. Open up the chicken like a book and lay it flat. (See how it looks like a butterfly?) Place it between two sheets of plastic wrap or in a resealable plastic bag. Using the bottom of a heavy pan, the smooth side of a meat mallet, or a rolling pin, pound the chicken breast to an even ¼-inch thickness. Repeat with the remaining breasts. Season the chicken all over with the salt and pepper.

2   Heat 2 tablespoons of the olive oil in a large skillet over medium-high heat. Place the flour in a wide, shallow dish. Dredge the butterflied chicken breasts in the flour to coat, shaking off any excess. When the oil is shimmering, add two of the dredged chicken breasts to the skillet and cook until golden brown and cooked through, 4 to 5 minutes per side. Transfer to a plate and tent with aluminum foil to keep warm. Heat the remaining 2 tablespoons oil in the pan and repeat with the remaining chicken.

3   Reduce the heat under the pan to medium, add the butter and garlic, and cook, stirring often, until fragrant, about 1 minute. Add the wine and cook, scraping up any browned bits from the bottom of the pan, for 2 to 3 minutes to cook off the alcohol (you'll be able to smell the difference); adjust the heat if the liquid is evaporating quickly. Add the stock, then the lemon zest and juice. Stir in the artichoke hearts and dill. Simmer for a few minutes to allow the flavors to meld. Stir in the cream and capers, and simmer until the sauce thickens slightly, another minute or two. Taste and season with salt and pepper.

4   Place the seared chicken breasts on a serving platter. Pour the sauce over the chicken, evenly distributing the artichoke hearts, dill, and capers. Garnish with dill and the lemon wedges for an extra pop of color and flavor. Enjoy on its own or over pasta, if you like!

French Onion Chicken Bake

Here we are taking a classic French dish and, dare I say, dumbing it down. Not that this recipe is dumb at all—it's just an alternate way to savor the flavors of the ever-iconic French onion soup (my all-time favorite). Succulent chicken (my other all-time favorite) is nestled in a bed of caramelized onions, bathed in a rich and flavorful sauce, and smothered in gooey broiled Gruyère. And I'll raise you one more: It's an easy-to-make one-pan bake. French onion soup may be timeless, but this recipe will take you way less time.

Serves 4

1 teaspoon kosher salt, plus more as needed

1 teaspoon onion powder

½ teaspoon freshly ground black pepper, plus more as needed

¼ teaspoon smoked paprika

4 boneless, skinless chicken breasts (6 to 8 ounces each)

4 tablespoons extra-virgin olive oil, plus more as needed

3 large yellow onions, thinly sliced

½ cup dry white wine (I like sauvignon blanc)

2 garlic cloves, minced or grated

1 tablespoon balsamic vinegar

1 tablespoon Worcestershire sauce

1 teaspoon dried thyme

1 teaspoon dried rosemary

1 teaspoon dried oregano

1 cup low-sodium chicken stock

1 cup heavy cream

1 cup freshly grated Gruyère cheese

Finely chopped fresh parsley, for serving

1   In a small bowl, stir together the salt, onion powder, pepper, and paprika. Season the chicken breasts on both sides with the spice mix and set aside to marinate for 30 minutes to 1 hour.

2   Meanwhile, heat 2 tablespoons of the olive oil in a large skillet over medium-high heat. When the oil is shimmering, add the onions and cook, stirring often, until they are beginning to take on some color, 5 to 7 minutes. Add the wine, season with salt, and reduce the heat to medium-low. Cook, stirring regularly, until brown and caramelized, about 30 minutes.

3   Preheat the oven to 375°F. Grease a 9×13-inch baking dish with olive oil.

4   Add the garlic to the caramelized onions and cook until fragrant, about 1 minute. Add the vinegar and Worcestershire and cook, scraping up any browned bits from the bottom of the skillet with a wooden spoon, until the sauce is incorporated into the onions, about 30 seconds. Add the thyme, rosemary, and oregano and season with salt and pepper. Transfer the onions to a plate.

5   Return the skillet to medium-high heat and add the remaining 2 tablespoons oil. When the oil is shimmering, add the chicken breasts and cook until a golden brown crust forms (they won't be cooked through yet), 2 to 3 minutes per side. Arrange the seared chicken breasts in the prepared baking dish in a single layer. Top the chicken with the caramelized onions, spreading them into an even layer.

6   Combine the stock and cream in a spouted measuring cup and pour the mixture over the chicken and onions in the baking dish. Bake for 25 to 30 minutes, until the chicken is cooked through (it should register 165°F on an instant-read thermometer) and the sauce has reduced slightly.

7   Sprinkle the Gruyère over the chicken breasts. Switch the oven to broil and cook until the cheese is melted, bubbling, and golden, about 3 minutes—be careful not to let it burn! Garnish with parsley and serve hot.

We're searing to develop a flavorful crust, NOT to fully cook the chicken. If you cook your chicken through too soon, it'll end up dry. Don't stress—it will finish cooking in the oven.

Olive You Braised Chicken

This cooking technique (low and slow) is kind of the antithesis of how I live my life (I tend to stay in the fast lane), but as I've mentioned before, we can learn a lot from the cooking process. The artful combination of fall-apart-tender chicken, nutty almonds, and briny olives is coaxed to perfection through deliberate braising. The slow life gives the flavors time to harmonize and deepen. If you're like me, navigating the chaos of a fast-paced existence, this recipe serves as a reminder savor the journey and to let life unfold at its own unhurried pace. The kitchen, like life, often rewards those who embrace the low and the slow, and I hope *olive you* taste the love in every bite.

Serves 4

1 cup whole almonds

3½ pounds bone-in, skin-on chicken thighs (6 to 8)

Kosher salt and freshly ground black pepper

2 tablespoons extra-virgin olive oil

1 large yellow onion, finely diced

4 garlic cloves, minced or grated

1 cup low-sodium chicken stock

½ cup canned diced tomatoes

½ cup pitted green olives (your choice) or Kalamata olives

½ teaspoon ground cumin

½ teaspoon sweet paprika

½ teaspoon ground turmeric

1 bay leaf

⅛ teaspoon cayenne pepper

Pinch of ground cinnamon

½ cup slivered almonds

Juice of ½ lemon, plus more as needed

Cooked couscous or rice, for serving (optional)

Finely chopped fresh parsley, for serving (optional)

1 In a food processor or blender, pulse the almonds into a fine, sandlike paste. Be careful not to go too far or you'll get almond butter!

2 Pat the chicken thighs dry with paper towels and season generously all over with salt and black pepper. Heat the olive oil in a large Dutch oven over medium-high heat. When the oil is shimmering, working in batches as needed, add the chicken thighs, skin-side down, and cook until golden brown and crispy, 5 to 10 minutes per side (don't worry about cooking them through yet). Transfer to a plate.

3 Pour off all but a tablespoon or so of the chicken fat from the pot and reduce the heat to medium. Add the onion and cook, stirring occasionally, until soft and translucent, about 4 minutes. Stir in the garlic and cook until fragrant, 1 minute. Add the ground almonds and cook, stirring often, to release the oils, about 2 minutes. Add the stock and the tomatoes with their juices and stir to combine. Add the olives, cumin, paprika, turmeric, bay leaf, cayenne, and cinnamon. Stir to incorporate.

4 Return the seared chicken thighs to the Dutch oven, nestling them into the sauce skin-side up, along with any collected juices. Bring the liquid to a gentle simmer. Cover the pot and adjust the heat as needed to keep the liquid at a very low simmer (just a few bubbles at a time). Simmer, stirring just a few times to prevent sticking, until the chicken is cooked through and the meat easily pulls away from the bone, 1½ to 2 hours.

Slow and steady wins the race; low and slow makes the braise.

5 Meanwhile, place the slivered almonds in a small skillet over medium heat. Toast, stirring often, until golden and fragrant, about 5 minutes—careful not to burn!

6 When the chicken is fully cooked, remove the Dutch oven from the heat. Add the lemon juice and stir to combine. Taste and adjust the seasoning to your liking; it should be deeply savory with just enough lemon and salt to make the other flavors shine. Serve the chicken and olives hot on their own, or over cooked couscous or rice. Top with the toasted almonds and fresh parsley, if desired.

Crispy Roast Chicken & Drippin' Panzanella

Double the recipe, double the trouble, double the fun. Not only is this a double recipe, but it also features a double dry-brining technique that helps pull out moisture from the chicken's skin, resulting in an ultra-crispy texture after roasting. This is a method I learned many years back by dining with my family at a quaint little spot in San Francisco called Zuni Café. It's named the "Judy Bird" method after the late, great chef Judy Rodgers. Just like Judy, you'll save the pan drippings to make the panzanella, and the bread will soak up that delicious chicken flavor—that's the double-fun part. Choose a loaf that is on the smaller side and has a great crust but a soft and chewy center. Be forewarned: You'll need to monitor the cooking process closely to achieve the perfect balance between crispy skin and juicy meat—that's the double-trouble part.

Serves 4 to 6

1 (3- to 4-pound) whole chicken

10 sprigs thyme

7 garlic cloves: 4 smashed and peeled, 3 thinly sliced

Kosher salt and freshly ground black pepper

3 tablespoons red wine vinegar

1 tablespoon warm water

1 tablespoon dried currants

7 tablespoons extra-virgin olive oil

4 scallions, sliced

1 small loaf slightly stale bread, torn into 2- to 3-inch chunks (about 4 cups)

2 teaspoons pine nuts, toasted

2 tablespoons low-sodium chicken stock, warmed, plus more as needed

3 handfuls arugula

1 Pat the chicken dry with paper towels and place it in a shallow dish (fitted with a wire rack if you've got one that will fit, but that's optional). Starting at the neck, separate the skin from each breast with your fingers and place the thyme and smashed garlic under the skin. Sprinkle salt evenly over the entire bird, focusing on the skin and using 1 teaspoon of salt per pound of chicken. Refrigerate the chicken, uncovered, for at least 24 hours or up to 72 hours.

2 Remove the chicken from the fridge. Tilt it to drain any juices from the cavity and pat it dry with paper towels. Let stand for 30 minutes to 1 hour before cooking to come to room temperature.

3 Meanwhile, preheat the oven to 475°F. Set a wire rack over a baking dish or baking sheet and place it in the oven to preheat as well.

4 After about 15 minutes, carefully remove the hot baking dish from the oven. Place the chicken on the rack, breast-side up; it should begin to sizzle immediately. Return the baking dish to the oven and reduce the oven temperature to 425°F. Roast the chicken for 50 to 60 minutes, until the internal temperature in the deepest part of the breast or thigh joint reaches 165°F. (I urge you to use a meat thermometer for this one to prevent over- or undercooking.) If the top of the chicken starts to brown too quickly, tent it with aluminum foil.

5 Meanwhile, in a small bowl, combine 1 tablespoon of the vinegar and the warm water. Add the currants and soak for 10 minutes. In a separate small bowl, whisk together 4 tablespoons of the olive oil with the remaining 2 tablespoons vinegar. Taste and season with salt and pepper to your liking.

HOT TIP Some chickens are juicier than others, so if you find you don't have enough drippings to use for the panzanella, deglaze the pan with some chicken stock and use that instead.

6 Heat 1 tablespoon of the olive oil in a small skillet over medium-low heat. When the oil is shimmering, add the sliced garlic and scallions, and cook, stirring continuously, until softened but still without color, about 4 minutes.

7 Remove the chicken from the oven and let rest for 10 to 15 minutes before carving. Save those pan juices! Switch the oven to broil.

8 On a baking sheet, toss the bread with the remaining 2 tablespoons olive oil. Broil for about 2 minutes, just to lightly color the edges.

9 Transfer the toasted bread to a serving bowl and toss with half the vinaigrette. Taste and adjust the seasoning to your liking. Scrape the garlic and scallions into the bowl with the bread and toss. Drain the currants and toss them in, too, along with the pine nuts.

10 Pour the warm stock evenly over the bread and toss. Drizzle with the chicken pan juices and toss again. The bread should not be totally soggy, but be sure no pieces are dry; add a little more stock if they are.

11 Add the arugula and the remaining vinaigrette. Toss, taste again, and season with salt and pepper to your liking. Divide the bread salad among plates or bowls, top with the roasted chicken, and serve.

Grilled Margarita Chicken

IT'S TEQUILA TIME! I can't lie—this recipe came to me when I was three margaritas deep, which makes me feel like I should drink margaritas more often. The marinade, a cocktail of tequila, lime juice, and orange juice, has the same effect on the chicken as it does on me—loosens it right up. Add a sprinkle of spice, and you've got yourself a recipe for the perfect night out—I mean, dinner.

Serves 4 to 6

½ cup tequila

Zest and juice of 2 limes

¼ cup fresh orange juice

¼ cup extra-virgin olive oil

¼ cup honey

3 garlic cloves, minced or grated

1 teaspoon chili powder

1 teaspoon smoked paprika

1 teaspoon kosher salt

½ teaspoon freshly ground black pepper

½ teaspoon ground cumin

¼ teaspoon cayenne pepper (optional)

8 bone-in, skin-on chicken pieces (I like to use a combination of thighs and drumsticks)

For Serving

Flaky salt

Fresh cilantro

Lime wedges

Reduce, reuse, reSAUCE. Don't toss the chicken marinade, bring it to a full boil (a very important step to kill any bacteria), then reduce the heat to reduce your marinade. CHEERS! You've made a delicious sauce for your meat.

1   In a measuring cup with a spout, combine the tequila, lime zest, lime juice, orange juice, olive oil, honey, garlic, chili powder, paprika, salt, black pepper, cumin, and cayenne (if using). Whisk to combine well.

2   Place the chicken in a large resealable plastic bag or a shallow dish. Pour the marinade over the chicken, turning the chicken to coat. Seal the bag or cover the dish and marinate in the refrigerator for at least 1 hour or up to 12 hours.

3   Heat your grill to medium-high or heat a grill pan over medium-high heat.

4   Remove the chicken pieces from the marinade (reserve the marinade!), allowing any excess to drip off, and place them on the grill. Grill the chicken until cooked through (it should register 165°F on an instant-read thermometer), 8 to 12 minutes per side, depending on the size of the pieces. Transfer the chicken to a serving platter and let it rest for a few minutes.

5   Meanwhile, pour the reserved marinade into a small saucepan. Bring to a boil over medium-high heat, then reduce the heat to medium-low and simmer until thickened and reduced, 5 to 10 minutes. Drizzle the reduced marinade over the chicken. Sprinkle with flaky salt and cilantro for a pop of color. Serve with lime wedges for an extra burst flavor.

Sheet Pan Chicken Shawarma

At Tasty, we were obsessed with using everyday kitchen tools to make cooking quicker, easier, cleaner, and subsequently more enjoyable. Sheet pans were one of those tools we hacked the heck out of. This recipe is more like a shawarma imposter than the real thing, but this sheet pan method yields a result that is just as delicious and a whole lot easier than MacGyver-ing an at-home spit. Trust me, it's the sheet.

Serves 4 to 6

½ cup plain full-fat Greek yogurt

2 tablespoons extra-virgin olive oil

3 garlic cloves, minced or grated

2 teaspoons ground cumin

1 teaspoon ground coriander

1 teaspoon smoked paprika

½ teaspoon ground turmeric

¼ teaspoon cayenne pepper

Kosher salt and freshly ground black pepper

Zest of ½ lemon

Juice of 1 lemon

1½ pounds boneless, skinless chicken thighs or breasts, cut into bite-size pieces

1 red bell pepper, thinly sliced

1 yellow bell pepper, thinly sliced

1 medium red onion, thinly sliced

For Serving

Finely chopped fresh dill or parsley

Pita bread or other flatbreads, warmed

Hummus, tzatziki (see page 185), pickles, sliced tomatoes, and/or sliced Persian cucumber (optional, but highly recommended)

1   In a large bowl or resealable plastic bag, stir together the yogurt, olive oil, garlic, cumin, coriander, paprika, turmeric, and cayenne. Season with salt and black pepper. Whisk in the lemon zest and juice until well combined. Taste and adjust the seasoning to your liking. Add the chicken to the marinade and toss to coat. Cover the bowl or seal the bag and marinate in the refrigerator for at least 30 minutes or (preferably) up to 2 hours.

2   Position an oven rack about 6 inches from the broiler heat source and preheat the oven to 425°F. Line a large baking sheet with parchment paper.

3   On the prepared baking sheet, spread out the red and yellow bell peppers and the onion. Roast for 15 minutes. Remove the baking sheet from the oven, stir the vegetables, and place the marinated chicken pieces on top, arranging them in a single layer. Roast for 15 to 20 minutes, stirring once, until the chicken is just barely cooked through and the vegetables are tender. Switch the oven to broil and cook until the chicken and vegetables are lightly caramelized, stirring once. Watch carefully to prevent burning!

4   Remove the pan from the oven and sprinkle everything with dill. I like to serve this straight from the baking sheet with warm pita bread. If you like, you can also add toppings like hummus, tzatziki, pickles, sliced tomatoes, and cucumber so everyone can customize their wraps.

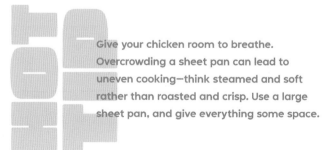

Give your chicken room to breathe. Overcrowding a sheet pan can lead to uneven cooking—think steamed and soft rather than roasted and crisp. Use a large sheet pan, and give everything some space.

Creamy Coconut Garlic Chicken Thighs

Between college and Tasty, I had absolutely no clue what to do with my life, so I moved to Sweden to work as an au pair. I lived with a family and helped take care of their two young boys. One of my tasks was cooking, and while the family expected only basic meals, I couldn't help but pull out all the stops. ("Au pair in Stockholm" was the closest I ever got to "private chef in the Hamptons.") The family was gluten- and dairy-free, and being that it was 2015, I had to get pretty damn creative in the kitchen. This recipe was one they requested on a weekly basis, probably thanks to its comfort, creaminess, and copious amounts of garlic.

Serves 4

3½ pounds bone-in, skin-on chicken thighs (6 to 8)

2 teaspoons kosher salt, plus more as needed

½ teaspoon freshly ground black pepper, plus more as needed

2 tablespoons extra-virgin olive oil

1 small yellow onion, finely diced

20 to 30 garlic cloves (from 2 to 3 heads), peeled

1 (14-ounce) can full-fat coconut milk

1 tablespoon curry powder

½ teaspoon ground turmeric

½ teaspoon ground cumin

¼ teaspoon cayenne pepper

Fresh cilantro or parsley, for serving

Cooked rice or warm naan, for serving

1   Pat the chicken thighs dry with paper towels and season them with the salt and black pepper. Heat the olive oil in a large skillet over medium-high heat. When the oil is shimmering, working in batches as needed, add the chicken skin-side down and cook until golden brown and crispy on the outside, about 5 minutes per side (it won't be cooked through yet). Transfer the chicken to a plate.

2   Pour off all but a tablespoon or so of the chicken fat from the pan and reduce the heat to medium. Add the onion and cook, stirring occasionally, until soft and translucent, about 5 minutes. Add the garlic and cook until fragrant, 1 minute. Pour in the coconut milk, stirring and scraping up any browned bits from the bottom of the pan. Add the curry powder, turmeric, cumin, and cayenne. Season with salt and black pepper and stir to combine everything.

3   Return the chicken thighs to the skillet, skin-side up, along with any juices that have collected on the plate, nestling them into the sauce. Bring the sauce to a gentle simmer, then reduce the heat to medium-low, cover, and cook until the chicken thighs are cooked through (they should register 165°F on an instant-read thermometer), about 25 minutes. Taste the sauce and adjust the seasoning to your liking.

4   Sprinkle the cilantro over the chicken. Serve over cooked rice or with warm naan bread on the side to soak up the delicious sauce.

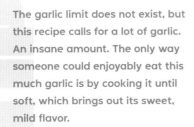

The garlic limit does not exist, but this recipe calls for a lot of garlic. An insane amount. The only way someone could enjoyably eat this much garlic is by cooking it until soft, which brings out its sweet, mild flavor.

Cheddar Chive Chicken 'n' Dumplins

What makes something "comfort food"? Is it the flavor? The nostalgia? The fuzzy feeling it brings? Or all of the above transforms a bunch of ingredients into a warm hug? Comfort foods are what I run to when life is hard and feelings are big. This dish right here is the epitome of comfort, a creamy filling crafted with love, aromatics, and tender chicken. The dumplings, enhanced with cheddar and chives, sit like fluffy pillows on top. There are foods that nourish the body and foods that nourish the soul. We all need both.

Serves 6

1 tablespoon extra-virgin olive oil

1 medium yellow onion, diced

2 medium carrots, diced

2 celery stalks, sliced

2 garlic cloves, minced or grated

Kosher salt and freshly ground black pepper

1¼ cups all-purpose flour

4 cups low-sodium chicken stock

1½ cups whole milk

2 cups shredded cooked chicken

1 cup frozen peas

1½ teaspoons baking powder

1½ cups freshly grated sharp cheddar cheese

¼ cup finely chopped fresh chives, plus more for serving

2 tablespoons unsalted butter, melted

Try not to eat the whole pot in one sitting.

1   Heat the olive oil in a large pot or Dutch oven over medium heat. When the oil is shimmering, add the onion, carrots, and celery. Cook, stirring occasionally, until the vegetables begin to soften, about 5 minutes. Stir in the garlic and cook until fragrant, another minute. Season with salt and pepper. Sprinkle ¼ cup of the flour over the vegetables and stir to coat. Cook, stirring continuously, until the raw flour taste has cooked out, about 1 minute.

2   Gradually pour in the stock and 1 cup of the milk while stirring continuously to avoid lumps. Bring the mixture to a simmer and cook, stirring occasionally, until the sauce thickens slightly, 5 to 7 minutes. Stir in the chicken and peas, and simmer until the chicken is heated through and the peas are tender, 5 minutes more. Taste and season with salt and pepper to your liking. Reduce the heat to maintain a simmer and cover the pot while you make the dumplings, stirring the stew occasionally.

3   In a medium bowl, whisk together the remaining 1 cup flour, the baking powder, 1 teaspoon salt, and ½ teaspoon pepper. Stir in 1 cup of the cheddar and the chives. Add the remaining ½ cup milk and the melted butter. Stir just until a thick and sticky dough forms—don't overmix!

4   Give the stew another stir to help ensure nothing sticks to the bottom. Drop spoonfuls of the dumpling dough on top, being sure to space them out. Sprinkle the remaining ½ cup cheddar over the dumplings. Cover the pot and cook, adjusting the heat as needed to maintain a simmer, until the dumplings are puffed up and cooked through and the cheese on top has melted, 12 to 15 minutes. Garnish with more chives and serve right away!

Beer-Battered Chicken Tenders
WITH HONEY-SRIRACHA SAUCE

Beer is to chicken tenders what honey is to sriracha: the perfect match. And it's time for a double date. The light and bubbly beer coating crisps up to create the most satisfying golden crust, which beautifully contrasts the juicy, tender chicken within. And before you call it a night, the tenders are dipped right into that irresistible kick of honey and sriracha. The only remaining question is, who's gonna foot the bill?

Serves 4

Vegetable oil, for frying

¼ cup honey

¼ cup sriracha

2 tablespoons low-sodium soy sauce

1 tablespoon extra-virgin olive oil

1 cup all-purpose flour

1 teaspoon baking powder

½ teaspoon kosher salt, plus more as needed

½ teaspoon freshly ground black pepper, plus more as needed

½ teaspoon garlic powder

½ teaspoon onion powder

½ teaspoon smoked paprika

1 cup light beer (I like pilsner)

1 large egg

8 chicken tenders (about 1 pound), or 1 pound chicken breasts, cut into 2-ounce strips

Sesame seeds, for serving

Excess flour in the dredge will turn gummy after frying, so cue the T. Swift and SHAKE IT OFF, SHAKE IT OFF.

1   Fill a large Dutch oven or heavy-bottomed pot halfway with vegetable oil. Clip a deep-fry thermometer to the side of the pot and heat the oil over medium-high heat until it reaches 350°F (see Hot Tip, page 79). Set a wire rack over a baking sheet or line a plate with paper towels.

2   In a small bowl, whisk together the honey, sriracha, soy sauce, and olive oil until well combined.

3   In a shallow bowl, whisk together the flour, baking powder, salt, pepper, garlic powder, onion powder, and paprika. In a separate shallow bowl, whisk together the beer and egg until well combined.

4   Season the chicken tenders with salt and pepper. Using one hand, dredge a tender in the flour mixture, gently shaking off any excess (see Hot Tip). Using the other hand, dip it in the beer mixture, allowing any excess to drip off. Dip once more in the flour, then the beer, again using one hand for the flour and the other for the beer mixture. Repeat with a few more tenders.

5   Working in batches, add the tenders to the hot oil and cook for 3 to 4 minutes per side, until golden brown, crispy, and cooked through (they should register 165°F on an instant-read thermometer). Use a slotted spoon or tongs to transfer the chicken tenders to the rack to drain. Repeat with the remaining tenders, allowing the oil to return to temperature between batches.

6   If you're serving the tenders immediately, brush them generously with the honey-sriracha sauce and sprinkle with sesame seeds. If you know they're going to sit, serve the sauce on the side for dipping so the breading doesn't get soggy. But don't wait more than 15 minutes—serve hot and enjoy!

SEAFOOD

Coconut Cornflake Shrimp

A fresh piña colada and crispy coconut shrimp—that's my perfect recipe for a tropical vacation. Yes, I happen to love coconut that much. You can't always live the leisurely life, so if you're stuck in your own kitchen and craving some good vibes, why not cook up a little slice of bliss? You already know I'm corny, so I threw some cornflakes into the coconut coating to tie everything together. They add a subtle sweetness that pairs swimmingly with the coconut, making a crispy, crunchy, and delightfully sweet bite that's even better with a delicious sweet chili dipping sauce. Close your eyes, take a bite, and let your taste buds whisk you away to paradise.

Serves 4

Vegetable oil, for frying

½ cup sweet chili sauce

1 tablespoon low-sodium soy sauce

1 tablespoon honey

Fresh lime juice, to taste

2 cups cornflakes

1 cup shredded coconut (sweetened or unsweetened, up to you)

1 cup all-purpose flour

½ teaspoon kosher salt, plus more as needed

¼ teaspoon freshly ground black pepper

¼ teaspoon cayenne pepper

2 large eggs

1 pound large shrimp, peeled and deveined

Lime wedges, for serving

This is deep-frying, not the deep sea—we don't want any mysteries. You want crunch, but you also still want to taste the delicate sweetness of the coconut and cornflakes. Be careful not to overfry or you'll dull those lovely flavors.

1 Fill a large deep skillet with 1 inch of oil. Clip a deep-fry thermometer to the side of the skillet and heat the oil over medium-high heat until it reaches 350°F (see Hot Tip, page 79). Line a plate with paper towels.

2 In a small bowl, whisk together the sweet chili sauce, soy sauce, honey, and lime juice to taste.

3 Place the cornflakes in a resealable plastic bag or food processor. Smash or pulse them into fine crumbs. Transfer to a shallow dish and stir in the coconut. In a separate shallow dish, combine the flour, salt, black pepper, and cayenne. Beat the eggs in a third shallow dish.

4 Working with one at a time, dredge a shrimp in the flour mixture, shaking off any excess, then dip it in the egg, allowing any excess to drip off (see Hot Tip, page 165). Dredge the shrimp in the cornflake mixture, pressing to adhere evenly on both sides. Transfer the coated shrimp to a plate and repeat with the remaining shrimp.

5 Working in batches to avoid crowding, add the coated shrimp to the hot oil and cook until golden and crispy, about 2 minutes per side. Watch carefully—don't let them get too dark!—and adjust the heat to keep the oil temperature steady. Use a slotted spoon to transfer them to the paper towel–lined plate to drain and season with salt. Repeat with the remaining shrimp, allowing the oil to return to temperature between batches.

6 Arrange the shrimp on a serving platter and serve right away, with lime wedges and the sauce alongside for dipping.

Champy Scampi

Truthfully, I'll take any excuse to enjoy a glass of Champagne, so why not add some CHAMPY to your SCAMPI? Excuse me if I've gone too far. Scampi-style is one of my favorite ways to eat shrimp, and bubbles make everything better. This is a recipe fit for the special-est of special occasions and elevates the classic dish to a new level of sophistication. Plump and juicy shrimp bathed in a velvety sauce that's infused with the effervescence of Champagne makes for a rich, buttery, sweet, and subtly luxe party of flavors—or should I say quiet luxury. Speaking of rich, grab the Champagne when you're feeling flush, or swap in Prosecco when you're not. No Champagne problems here.

Serves 4

Kosher salt

12 ounces long-cut pasta (I like linguine or spaghetti)

1 pound large shrimp, peeled and deveined

1¼ cups Champagne or other sparkling white wine

1 tablespoon extra-virgin olive oil

4 garlic cloves, minced or grated

¼ teaspoon red pepper flakes

¼ cup heavy cream

Freshly ground black pepper

2 tablespoons unsalted butter

Zest and juice of 1 lemon

2 tablespoons finely chopped fresh parsley, for serving

Lemon wedges, for serving

HOT TIP

Don't forget to pour yourself a glass of Champagne (or two) while cooking! Now *that's* a hot tip.

1   Bring a large pot of water to a boil over high heat. Salt the water so it's salty like the tears of happiness you will cry when you taste this dish. Add the pasta and cook until al dente according to the package directions. Reserve about 1 cup of the pasta cooking water, then drain the pasta.

2   Meanwhile, in a medium bowl, combine the shrimp and 1 cup of the Champagne. Set aside to marinate at room temperature for 15 to 20 minutes.

3   Heat the olive oil in a large skillet over medium heat. When the oil is shimmering, add the garlic and red pepper flakes and cook, stirring often, until the garlic is fragrant, about 1 minute.

4   Use tongs or a slotted spoon to transfer the shrimp to a plate. Pour 1 cup of the Champagne (yes, it's the color of shrimp right now—don't think about it too hard) into the saucepan with the garlic and bring it to a gentle simmer. Cook until reduced slightly, 3 to 4 minutes. Add the cream and cook, stirring often, until the sauce thickens slightly, 2 to 3 minutes more. Season with salt and black pepper.

5   Reduce the heat to medium-low, add the butter, and stir to melt. Stir in the remaining ¼ cup Champagne, the lemon zest, and the lemon juice. Taste and adjust the seasoning to your liking. Add the shrimp and cook, stirring often, until the shrimp are just opaque, about 1 minute.

6   Add the pasta and toss vigorously to coat. Cook until the shrimp are pink and cooked through and the sauce coats the pasta evenly, about 2 minutes, then remove from the heat. Sprinkle with the parsley and serve hot, with lemon wedges alongside for squeezing.

Scallops Piccata

I have to admit something: Seafood is not my favorite. I had a seafood aversion as a kid, and while I have moved far past that era of my life, I still reach for pretty much anything else first. I cook for a living, but I rarely cook seafood, *especially* since Zoya owns a vegan fish company. This recipe was something I developed to let seafood in a little more. I love chicken piccata (see page 147), and I knew the briny and buttery flavors of the classic dish would pair well with briny and buttery scallops. If I can thoroughly enjoy this recipe, I know you will, too. It's a lighter meal on its own, so I suggest pairing it with pasta to tide you over (get it?).

Serves 4

2 tablespoons all-purpose flour

1 pound fresh sea scallops, tough ligament removed

Kosher salt and freshly ground black pepper

2 tablespoons extra-virgin olive oil

2 garlic cloves, minced or grated

¼ cup dry white wine (I like sauvignon blanc)

¼ cup low-sodium chicken stock or vegetable stock

Juice of 1 lemon

2 tablespoons drained capers

2 tablespoons unsalted butter

2 tablespoons finely chopped fresh parsley, for serving

1 lemon, halved and thinly sliced, for serving

1 Place the flour on a small plate. Pat the scallops very dry with paper towels, then season generously all over with salt and pepper. Lightly dip the tops and bottoms of the scallops in the flour to coat, shaking off any excess.

2 Heat the olive oil in a large skillet over medium-high heat. When the oil is shimmering, working in batches as needed to avoid overcrowding, add the scallops and cook, undisturbed, until a golden brown crust forms, 2 to 3 minutes on each side. Take care not to overcook them, as they can become chewy! Transfer to a plate and tent with aluminum foil to keep warm. Repeat with the remaining scallops.

3 Reduce the heat to medium and add the garlic to the skillet. Cook, stirring, until fragrant, about 30 seconds. Pour in the wine and cook, scraping up any browned bits from the bottom of the skillet, until reduced slightly (reduce the heat as needed if it's cooking too fast), 1 to 2 minutes. Pour in the stock and lemon juice. Bring the mixture to a simmer and cook until the flavors have melded, 5 to 6 minutes.

4 Stir in the capers and butter. Cook until the butter has melted and the sauce has thickened slightly, about 1 minute. Taste and adjust the seasoning to your liking. Return the scallops to the skillet and spoon the sauce over them. Scatter the parsley and lemon slices over everything and serve right away.

Scallops are meant to be seared, so don't be scared of developing that golden crust.

Crab Rangoon Cakes
WITH SWEET CHILI SAUCE

You may recall crab rangoon had a moment of social media fame. To celebrate, we're making CAKE. Crab cakes, that is, with a rangoon tune. This recipe blends luxurious crab with the beloved flavors of crab rangoon (aka velvety cream cheese), all wrapped up in a crispy coating akin to that of a crab shell. No candles necessary—we're serving these cakes up with the bold flavors of the retro classic: sweet chili sauce.

Serves 4 to 6

Crab Cakes

1 cup panko breadcrumbs

⅓ cup cream cheese, at room temperature

1 large egg

1 tablespoon low-sodium soy sauce

1 tablespoon sweet chili sauce

1 teaspoon Worcestershire sauce

1 teaspoon toasted sesame oil

1 teaspoon sugar

½ teaspoon garlic powder

2 garlic cloves, minced or grated

Kosher salt and freshly ground black pepper

1 pound lump crabmeat

2 scallions, thinly sliced

Vegetable oil, for frying

Sweet Chili Sauce

¼ cup sweet chili sauce

1 tablespoon low-sodium soy sauce

1 teaspoon rice vinegar

½ teaspoon toasted sesame oil

For Serving

Toasted sesame seeds

Fresh cilantro

1 Make the crab cakes. In a large bowl, stir together ¼ cup of the panko, the cream cheese, egg, soy sauce, sweet chili sauce, Worcestershire, sesame oil, sugar, garlic powder, and garlic and season with salt and pepper. Add the crabmeat and scallions. Gently fold the ingredients together to combine well and evenly; the mixture will be very wet. Taste and adjust the seasoning to your liking (or fry a tiny portion of the mixture and taste that, if raw egg freaks you out).

2 Divide the crab mixture into 12 equal portions and shape each into a patty, ½ to ¾ inch thick. Place the remaining ¾ cup panko in a shallow dish. Carefully coat each crab cake all over in the breadcrumbs, pressing gently to adhere and reshaping the crab cakes as needed (the panko will help them hold their shape).

3 Coat the bottom of a large skillet with a thin layer of vegetable oil and heat over medium heat. Line a plate with paper towels. When the oil is shimmering, working in batches as needed, carefully add the crab cakes and cook until golden brown and crispy, 2 to 5 minutes per side, adjusting the heat if they're browning too fast. Carefully transfer the crab cakes to the paper towels to drain. Repeat with the remaining crab cakes, adding more oil between batches as needed.

4 Make the sauce. In a small bowl, whisk together the sweet chili sauce, soy sauce, vinegar, and sesame oil.

5 Arrange the crab rangoon cakes on a platter, sprinkle with sesame seeds and cilantro, and serve hot, with the sauce on the side for drizzling.

When shaping your crab into a patty—dare I say, a crabby patty?—wet your hands a little first so the mixture doesn't stick.

Firework Salmon

Are you ready for a flavor EXPLOSION? This is my take on the classic firecracker chicken because, personally, I prefer fire*works*. Loud and bold, a delicate balance of sweet and spicy—this salmon and I have a lot in common. Marinated to perfection with a dynamic mixture of soy sauce, honey, Dijon mustard, sriracha, and more—the salmon is sparked up under the broiler, creating both charred edges and tender flesh. Be careful using the broiler, because just like a firework, things will heat up *fast*. I only have one question: Do you ever feel like a plastic bag?

Serves 4

¼ cup low-sodium soy sauce

2 tablespoons honey

2 tablespoons Dijon mustard

2 tablespoons toasted sesame oil

1 tablespoon sriracha

2 garlic cloves, minced or grated

1 tablespoon grated fresh ginger

Zest and juice of 1 lime

4 (6-ounce) salmon fillets

Kosher salt and freshly ground black pepper

For Serving

Sliced scallions

Sesame seeds

Lime wedges

1   In a small bowl, whisk together the soy sauce, honey, Dijon, sesame oil, sriracha, garlic, ginger, lime zest, and lime juice.

2   Season the salmon fillets with salt and pepper. Arrange them in a single layer in a shallow dish or large resealable plastic bag. Pour over half the marinade, ensuring each fillet is generously coated; reserve the remaining marinade. Cover the dish or seal the bag and set aside to marinate at room temperature for 30 minutes to 1 hour.

3   Position an oven rack about 6 inches from the broiler heat source and preheat the broiler. Line a baking sheet with aluminum foil and set a wire rack on top.

4   Arrange the salmon on the prepared baking sheet, brushing the fillets with a little of the reserved marinade. Broil for about 15 minutes, until the edges are slightly charred and the thickest part of the salmon flakes easily with a fork. Remove from the oven, transfer the fillets to a serving platter, and set aside to rest.

5   Pour the remaining reserved marinade into a small saucepan and cook over medium heat, stirring often, until reduced and thickened slightly, about 3 minutes.

6   Drizzle the reduced marinade over the fillets and sprinkle with scallions and sesame seeds. Serve with lime wedges alongside.

I wrote you a little poem: When the salmon's opaque and with a fork you can flake, your salmon is done, for goodness' sake.

Garlic Confit Poached Salmon

Poaching salmon in olive oil is a gentle cooking technique that yields the most delicate and luscious texture—but why stop there? I'm always trying to push the boundaries of a recipe just like I like to push boundaries in life. Garlic confit uses that same gentle cooking technique to make garlic cloves that are soft, tender, and sweet. It's not the fastest process to achieve that end result, but by starting on the stove and finishing in the oven, I've managed to save you a few minutes. You'll have one more dish to clean, but you can wash it and then some in the time you'll save. This cooking method will preserve the salmon's pink color, so your fish may appear rarer than you're used to. To check for doneness, flake the fish with a fork or use a thermometer to check the internal temp; you're looking for 120°F for medium-rare.

Serves 4

12 garlic cloves
(from 1 head)

1 cup extra-virgin olive oil

4 (6-ounce) salmon
fillets, as even thickness
as possible (see Hot Tip),
skin removed

Kosher salt and freshly
ground black pepper

4 to 6 sprigs thyme

½ lemon, thinly sliced

Juice of ½ lemon

Flaky salt, for serving

1   Place the garlic cloves in a small saucepan and cover them with the olive oil. Cook over low heat until the cloves are tender, 20 to 25 minutes. You want just a few bubbles at a time, so adjust the heat as needed, and take care not to let the garlic brown at all. Remove the pan from the heat and let cool for 30 minutes to allow the flavors to intensify.

2   Meanwhile, position a rack in the center of the oven and preheat to 225°F.

3   Season the salmon fillets with salt and pepper on both sides and place them in a single layer in a 9 × 13-inch baking dish. Pour the olive oil and garlic over the top, submerging the fish about halfway. Top the salmon with half the thyme, then lay the lemon slices on top.

4   Bake the salmon for about 18 minutes for thin fillets and up to 30 minutes for thick ones, until the thickest part of the salmon flakes easily with a fork.

5   Transfer the salmon fillets to plates and drizzle some of the garlic-infused oil over each. Garnish with all the poached garlic cloves (they won't keep!), then top with the remaining thyme and drizzle the lemon juice all over. Sprinkle with flaky salt and enjoy!

HOT TIP

Fish fillets, like people, come in all shapes and sizes. Because we're looking for a just-cooked tender texture, choose fillets that are an even thickness. They'll cook at the same rate throughout, leaving you with no under- or overcooked parts.

Green Curry Cod

This green curry cod is probably my personal favorite way to eat fish, and that means a lot coming from me. White fish like cod are mild in flavor, so the sauce carries the team, and it does so almost effortlessly here. Store-bought green curry paste is convenient but can lack the depth of flavor of a homemade version, so I hack it with fish sauce, lime juice, and sugar. The delicate fillets swim in the gentle sweetness of coconut, the fragrant zest of lemongrass, and the tempered heat of Thai chiles. It'll have you hooked from the first bite.

Serves 4

4 (6-ounce) cod fillets, as even thickness as possible

Kosher salt and freshly ground black pepper

1 tablespoon extra-virgin olive oil

1 medium yellow onion, sliced

2 tablespoons green curry paste

1 red bell pepper, sliced

1 medium head bok choy, trimmed and coarsely chopped

1 (13.5-ounce) can full-fat coconut milk

2 tablespoons fish sauce, plus more as needed

1 tablespoon light brown sugar, plus more as needed

Juice of ½ lime, plus more as needed

Cooked jasmine rice, for serving

Fresh Thai basil leaves or cilantro leaves, for serving

1 Season the cod all over with salt and black pepper.

2 Heat the olive oil in a large skillet over medium heat. When the oil is shimmering, add the onion and cook, stirring occasionally, until soft and translucent, about 7 minutes. Add the curry paste and cook, stirring more frequently, until fragrant, about 1 minute. Add the bell pepper and bok choy and cook, stirring often, until the vegetables begin to soften, 3 to 4 minutes. Season with salt and black pepper. Pour in the coconut milk and stir well. Bring the mixture to a simmer and cook for about 5 minutes to allow the flavors to meld.

3 Stir in the fish sauce, brown sugar, and lime juice. Taste and adjust the seasoning to your liking. Gently place the cod in the sauce and spoon some over the fillets. Cover the pan and simmer until the fish is cooked through and flakes easily with a fork at its thickest point, 5 to 7 minutes.

4 Remove the pan from the heat. Divide the rice among four plates, add the cod, and spoon the sauce over everything. Garnish with basil leaves and serve immediately.

Store-bought ingredients like green curry paste can vary widely, so keep in mind that the amounts provided are merely suggestions. Taste as you go and adjust to suit your palate, especially if you want to pack on the heat!

Black & White Fish
WITH SWEET CORN SUCCOTASH

Black and white fish or blackened white fish—no matter the title, this dish is far from coy (or should I say, *koi*?). In fact, it will punch you in the mouth with flavor, but, like, in the best way. The tender fish gets a (very) spicy and smoky coating that blackens with the heat, while that corn succotash steps in to cool everything down with a beautiful brightness and sweetness. Beware that while this dish is bold, the fish is delicate, so be sure to handle the fillets carefully while preparing.

Serves 4

Succotash

2 tablespoons unsalted butter

1 red bell pepper, diced

1 small red onion, diced

2 cups frozen sweet corn kernels

1 cup cherry tomatoes, halved

Juice of ½ lemon, plus more if needed

Kosher salt and freshly ground black pepper

Fish

4 (6-ounce) white fish fillets such as tilapia, snapper, or cod

1 tablespoon smoked paprika

1 tablespoon onion powder

1 teaspoon cayenne pepper

1 teaspoon garlic powder

1 teaspoon freshly ground black pepper

1 teaspoon kosher salt

½ teaspoon dried basil

½ teaspoon dried oregano

½ teaspoon dried thyme

2 tablespoons extra-virgin olive oil

2 tablespoons finely chopped fresh dill, parsley, or cilantro, for serving

1   Make the succotash. Melt the butter in a large skillet over medium heat. Add the bell pepper and onion and cook, stirring occasionally, until beginning to soften, 3 to 4 minutes. Add the corn and cook, stirring occasionally, until tender, 3 to 4 minutes. Stir in the tomatoes and cook until slightly softened, 1 to 2 minutes. Add the lemon juice and stir to combine. Season with salt and black pepper. Taste and adjust the seasoning to your liking. Transfer to a medium bowl and cover to keep warm. Wipe out the skillet.

2   Make the fish. Pat the fillets dry with paper towels.

3   In a small bowl, stir together the paprika, onion powder, cayenne, garlic powder, black pepper, salt, basil, oregano, and thyme. Rub each fillet all over with 1 tablespoon of the seasoning mix, ensuring they are coated evenly.

4   In the skillet you used for the succotash, heat the olive oil over medium-high heat. When the oil is shimmering, add the fish and cook until the spice coating is blackened and the fish is cooked through, flakes easily with a fork, and releases from the pan without resistance, 2 to 4 minutes per side.

5   To serve, divide the succotash among four plates and add one fish fillet to each. Garnish with dill and serve right away.

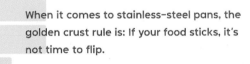

When it comes to stainless-steel pans, the golden crust rule is: If your food sticks, it's not time to flip.

White Fish Souvlaki
WITH TZATZIKI

After spending two consecutive summers hopping between the Greek islands, it's hard to pick a highlight—scratch that, no, it's not. It's the souvlaki, hands down. Let me tell you, I averaged two a day. Yup, so SOU ME! This recipe is inspired by the zesty, herbaceous, and garlicky flavors that are forever skewered in my memory. While traditional souvlaki pairs beautifully with meat, I find that fish is too delicate for skewers. Instead, I've ditched both the skewers and the grill. After a few failed attempts, I turned to the oven and discovered that using a foil-wrapped pan and the broiler creates the characteristic charred flavor and color. With this method, you can avoid broken fish—and a broken heart!

Serves 4

¼ cup extra-virgin olive oil

Juice of 1 lemon

4 garlic cloves, minced or grated

1 teaspoon dried oregano

½ teaspoon dried thyme

½ teaspoon dried rosemary

Kosher salt and freshly ground black pepper

4 (4-ounce) white fish fillets, such as cod, halibut, or tilapia, as even thickness as possible

½ Persian cucumber

1 cup plain full-fat Greek yogurt

1 tablespoon finely chopped fresh dill or mint, plus more for serving

1   In an 8- or 9-inch square dish, whisk together the olive oil, half the lemon juice, half the garlic, the oregano, thyme, and rosemary and season with salt and pepper. Taste and adjust the seasoning to your liking—it should be punchy! Add the fish in a single layer and gently turn to coat evenly. Cover and marinate in the refrigerator for at least 30 minutes or up to 2 hours.

2   Meanwhile, grate the cucumber into a clean towel. Holding the towel over the sink, squeeze out as much liquid from the cucumber as you can. Place the squeezed cucumber in a medium bowl and stir in the yogurt, the remaining garlic, remaining lemon juice, and the dill to combine well. Season the tzatziki with salt and pepper to your liking. Cover and refrigerate the tzatziki for at least 30 minutes or up to 24 hours before serving.

3   Position an oven rack about 6 inches from the broiler heat source and preheat the broiler. Line a baking sheet with aluminum foil and set a wire rack on top.

4   Remove the fish fillets from the marinade, allowing any excess to drip off, and transfer them to the prepared pan. Broil for about 7 minutes for very thin fish like tilapia and up to 15 minutes for thick fish like cod, until the fish is cooked through and lightly charred on top, and flakes easily with a fork at its thickest point.

5   Use a spatula to carefully transfer the fish to a serving platter. Sprinkle with more fresh herbs and serve with the tzatziki on the side.

You want your fish to char a bit, so be sure to allow that excess marinade to drip off before broiling.

Fish Puttanesca

Cooking seafood can be intimidating, so straightforward and simple is the name of the game, and each and every seafood recipe I have to offer you is salt of the earth, or better yet—the sea. Fish cooks more quickly than other proteins, which means it's prone to being *overcooked*, so it's best to keep a close eye on it—good thing eating fish is good for eye health! Puttanesca is a relatively simple Italian sauce made with anchovies, olives, capers, and a chunky tomato base. It's bright and briny, and comes together as quickly as the fish cooks within it, resulting in a dish that's shore to make a splash. (SOMEBODY STOP ME, PLEASE.)

Serves 4

4 (4-ounce) skinless white fish fillets, such as cod, halibut, or tilapia

Kosher salt and freshly ground black pepper

2 tablespoons extra-virgin olive oil

1 small yellow onion, diced

3 garlic cloves, minced or grated

3 anchovy fillets, minced, or ½ teaspoon anchovy paste (optional)

1 (14-ounce) can diced tomatoes, with their juices

½ cup pitted Kalamata olives, halved

2 tablespoons drained capers

¼ teaspoon red pepper flakes

¼ cup dry white wine (I like sauvignon blanc)

Cooked pasta or crusty bread, for serving

Fresh parsley, for serving

1   Pat the fish dry with paper towels and season with salt and black pepper on both sides.

2   Heat the olive oil in a large skillet over medium heat. When the oil is shimmering, add the onion and cook, stirring occasionally, until softened and translucent, about 7 minutes. Stir in the garlic and cook until fragrant, 1 minute. Add the anchovies (if using) and stir until they've dissolved, 1 to 2 minutes.

3   Add the tomatoes with their juices and use the back of your spoon to break them down a bit so they get a little saucy-meets-chunky. Stir in the olives, capers, and red pepper flakes. Pour in the wine. Return the mixture to a simmer, then reduce the heat to medium-low, cover, and simmer until the flavors have melded and the sauce has thickened slightly, about 10 minutes. Taste and adjust the seasoning to your liking.

4   Gently place the fish in the sauce. Spoon some of the sauce over the fillets to coat. Cover the pan and cook for 6 to 10 minutes, until the fish is opaque, cooked through, and flakes easily with a fork at its thickest point. Taste the sauce and adjust the seasoning to your liking.

5   Remove the pan from the heat. Serve the fish puttanesca over cooked pasta or with crusty bread to soak up the delicious sauce, dividing it among four plates. Garnish with parsley and serve.

If anchovies freak you out, you can leave them out. If you do choose to use them, be mindful of their natural saltiness; you might not need to use as much actual salt in the dish.

BEEF, PORK, AND LAMB

Honey-Whiskey Ribs

On my twenty-second birthday, I cried over a plate of ribs. I don't remember why, but I do remember my friends took me to get ribs in a desperate attempt to cheer me up. Instead of blowing out twenty-two candles, I ate twenty-two ribs (even better). Long story short, it worked: Whether you make these on a grill or in the oven, they will lip-smack you right out of the blues with a delectable honey-whiskey glaze. Remember, if you rush the ribs, you'll end up with tough meat stuck to the bone versus juicy meat that falls off the bone. They are a time investment, but we all know good ribs come to those who wait.

SERVES 6 TO 10

4 to 5 pounds baby back ribs

1 tablespoon smoked paprika

2 teaspoons onion powder

2 teaspoons garlic powder

2 teaspoons mustard powder

1½ teaspoons light brown sugar

1 teaspoon cayenne pepper

1 teaspoon kosher salt

½ teaspoon freshly ground black pepper

½ cup honey

¼ cup whiskey or bourbon (or whiskey-adjacent spirit)

¼ cup ketchup

2 tablespoons low-sodium soy sauce

2 tablespoons apple cider vinegar

2 garlic cloves, minced or grated

1 teaspoon Dijon mustard

Indirect grilling is essentially using your grill as an oven. Keep the charcoal (or burners) on one side, and start the ribs on the cooler side to cook them low and slow. When they're ready, move them over to the hot side for a perfect char!

1   Heat the grill to medium for indirect cooking (see Hot Tip) or preheat the oven to 300°F. If using the oven, line a baking sheet with aluminum foil.

2   Start by removing the membrane from the back of the ribs, if you want to. Some butchers may remove them first, or score the back to help with this, but if yours has not, use a knife to loosen the white membrane at one end of the rack. Grip it with a paper towel and peel it off completely. If your ribs are too big to fit onto a sheet pan or to handle easily, cut them into smaller racks.

3   In a small bowl, combine the paprika, onion powder, garlic powder, mustard powder, brown sugar, cayenne, salt, and black pepper. Sprinkle the spice mixture onto the ribs and massage it into both sides.

4   In a small saucepan, whisk together the honey, whiskey, ketchup, soy sauce, vinegar, garlic, and Dijon. Bring to a simmer over medium heat. Reduce the heat to medium-low and cook, stirring occasionally, until the glaze thickens slightly, 8 to 10 minutes. Taste and season with salt and black pepper to your liking. Remove the pan from the heat.

5   To grill the ribs, place them on the grill over burner(s) that aren't turned on. Close the lid and cook for 1½ to 2 hours, until the ribs are tender and the meat begins to pull away from the bones. To bake the ribs, place them on the prepared baking sheet and cover tightly with aluminum foil. Bake for 2½ to 3 hours, until the ribs are tender when pierced with a knife and the meat is practically falling off the bone.

6   During the last 10 minutes of cooking, when the ribs are nearly done, move them to the hot side of the grill and brush the glaze over the ribs, turning them once. If using the oven, remove the foil, brush with the glaze, and switch the oven to broil for the last 5 minutes to caramelize, watching carefully to prevent burning. Remove the ribs from the grill or oven and allow them to rest for 5 minutes before slicing into individual portions.

7   Serve the ribs with any remaining glaze alongside!

Pistachio & Feta-Stuffed Lamb Meatballs

WITH TOMATO-YOGURT SAUCE

Meatballs are one of my top five favorite foods, and I love them in all their iterations. It's not just because they're delicious. There's just something inherently charming about food in the shape of a ball. Round, stuffed, and utterly irresistible. Here we've got juicy and savory lamb, the surprise crunch of pistachios, and creamy, tangy feta rolled into little flavor bombs served with the most luxurious tomato-yogurt sauce. If you're not a fan of lamb, you can swap in ground beef or even turkey or chicken. Round up your ingredients and get ready to roll, because it's time for mouth to meet ball.

SERVES 4

Meatballs

1 pound ground lamb

½ cup panko breadcrumbs

¼ cup finely chopped fresh parsley

¼ cup finely chopped fresh mint leaves

¼ cup finely chopped pistachios, plus more for serving

¼ cup finely chopped red onion

2 garlic cloves, minced or grated

1 teaspoon ground cumin

1 teaspoon kosher salt

½ teaspoon freshly ground black pepper

½ teaspoon ground coriander

2 ounces feta cheese, cut or crumbled into 16 small pieces

Extra-virgin olive oil

Tomato-Yogurt Sauce

⅓ cup plain full-fat Greek yogurt

3 tablespoons canned tomato sauce or crushed tomatoes

Fresh lemon juice

1 teaspoon finely chopped fresh dill, plus more for serving

Kosher salt and freshly ground black pepper

Flaky salt, for serving

1 **Make the meatballs.** In a large bowl, combine the lamb, breadcrumbs, parsley, mint, pistachios, onion, garlic, cumin, salt, pepper, and coriander. Using your hands, mix until just combined.

2 Scoop up about 2 tablespoons of the lamb mixture and flatten it in your palm. Place a small piece of feta in the center, then wrap the lamb mixture around the cheese to form a meatball and seal the opening. Repeat with the remaining meat mixture and cheese. Don't overstuff your meatballs, and be sure to seal them well or they may explode! You should have about 16 meatballs.

3 Coat the bottom of a large skillet with olive oil and heat over medium heat. When the oil is shimmering, working in batches, add the meatballs and cook, carefully turning them, until they are browned all over, 8 to 10 minutes total. Transfer to a serving platter to rest for about 5 minutes and repeat with the remaining meatballs.

4 **Make the tomato-yogurt sauce.** In a medium bowl, whisk together the yogurt, tomato sauce, a squeeze of lemon juice, and the dill and season with salt and pepper. Taste and adjust the seasoning to your liking.

5 Drizzle the tomato-yogurt sauce over the meatballs or serve it in a bowl alongside for dipping. Garnish with dill and pistachios and a sprinkle of flaky salt.

HOT TIP

You need to cook the meatballs on all sides—wait, do balls even have sides? You can flip each one with tongs or shake the pan to roll them around the pan for allover browning.

Beef Bulgogi Bowls

I've been lucky enough to travel a lot in my life, but I have yet to go to Korea. Technically speaking, I had a layover in Seoul once, but I didn't step foot outside the airport, so I don't think that counts. That hasn't stopped me from exploring the food. Korean food is incredibly delicious, with its bold flavors, a focus on fermentation, and don't even get me started on how good KBBQ is (especially here in LA!). Bulgogi is one of my all-time favorites, with tender slices of marinated beef paired with a medley of fresh vegetables, all served atop a bed of fluffy rice. This dish is a delicate balance of sweet and savory, with hints of garlic and soy—I'm already drooling. Let's take a journey into Korean cuisine together. The aromas that fill your kitchen will carry you away to a place where worries are minced finer than garlic.

SERVES 4

½ cup low-sodium soy sauce

½ Asian pear, cored and finely grated

¼ cup toasted sesame seeds, plus more for serving

2 tablespoons packed light or dark brown sugar

2 tablespoons toasted sesame oil

2 tablespoons rice vinegar

1 tablespoon gochujang or chili garlic sauce

1 tablespoon grated fresh ginger

4 garlic cloves, minced or grated

1 pound very thinly sliced rib eye or sirloin steak (see Hot Tip)

2 tablespoons vegetable oil

Kosher salt

1 medium yellow onion, sliced

3 medium carrots, cut into thin matchsticks

4 cups cooked rice

2 Persian cucumbers, thinly sliced

2 radishes, thinly sliced

4 scallions, sliced

4 fried eggs (optional)

Your favorite chili sauce, for serving (optional)

1 In a medium bowl, combine the soy sauce, grated pear, sesame seeds, brown sugar, sesame oil, rice vinegar, gochujang, ginger, and garlic. Whisk until the sugar has dissolved. Add the beef and turn to coat well. Cover the bowl and marinate in the refrigerator for at least 1 hour or up to overnight.

2 Heat the vegetable oil in a large skillet or wok over high heat. When the oil is shimmering, working in batches as needed, remove the beef from the marinade, allowing any excess to drip off, add it to the pan, and immediately reduce the heat to medium-high. Season with salt. Cook the beef, stirring regularly, until it's cooked through and caramelized, about 3 minutes. Transfer the beef to a plate and repeat with the remaining meat.

3 In the same skillet (if there are any really charred bits on the bottom, scrape those off, but no need to clean it), cook the onion, stirring occasionally, until soft and translucent, 3 to 4 minutes. Add the carrots and cook until slightly tender, about 2 minutes more. Transfer to the plate with the beef.

4 Divide the rice among four bowls. Arrange the beef, onion and carrots, cucumber, radish, and scallions on top. Sprinkle more sesame seeds over everything. If desired, top each bowl with a fried egg and season the egg with a bit of salt. Serve immediately, with chili sauce alongside, if you like.

If you can't find presliced steak, freeze the meat for 1 to 2 hours before slicing. When the steak is partially frozen, it's much easier to cut thin, even slices—and it will thaw quickly once sliced.

Balsamic-Marinated Steak
WITH CHIMICHURRI PESTO

Call me crazy if you want, but I have never liked store-bought pesto. Or any pesto, for that matter. In my humble opinion, it lacks acidity, freshness, and bite. That's why, one day, while eating chimichurri with steak, I thought, *THIS! This is what pesto is lacking.* And BAM! My chimichurri pesto was born. (I live for lightbulb moments like that.) What pesto lacks in complexity, this sauce makes up for. The punch from the shallot and vinegar and the richness from the oil, nuts, and cheese play together so effortlessly. It has now become my all-time favorite meat companion, especially for this balsamic-marinated steak. Think of this hybrid sauce and perfectly seared steak like soulmates, twin flames, the perfect match. So meant for each other, it'll have you believing in fate.

SERVES 4

Steak

¼ cup balsamic vinegar

2 tablespoons extra-virgin olive oil

2 garlic cloves, minced or grated

1 teaspoon dried thyme

Kosher salt and freshly ground black pepper

4 (6-ounce) rib eye steaks, about 1½ inches thick

Chimichurri Pesto

1 medium shallot, chopped

1 cup packed fresh parsley

½ cup packed fresh basil leaves

⅓ cup freshly grated Parmigiano Reggiano cheese

¼ cup pine nuts or walnuts

¼ cup extra-virgin olive oil

¼ cup red wine vinegar

3 garlic cloves, peeled

Kosher salt and freshly ground black pepper

Red pepper flakes (optional)

1   **Make the steak.** In a small bowl, whisk together the balsamic vinegar, olive oil, garlic, and thyme and generously season with salt and black pepper. Place the steaks in a resealable plastic bag or a shallow dish in a single layer. Pour in the marinade, coating the steaks evenly. Seal the bag or cover the dish and marinate in the refrigerator for 1 to 2 hours.

2   Heat your grill to high or heat a large cast-iron skillet over high heat.

3   Remove the steaks from the marinade, letting any excess drip off, and place them on the grill or grill pan. Cook, flipping them frequently, until done to your liking, about 7 minutes total for medium-rare or about 9 minutes for medium. Remove the steaks when they reach 130°F for medium-rare and 140°F for medium. (Rib eye steak is best cooked to medium-rare or medium for optimal tenderness; see Hot Tip.) Transfer the steaks to a cutting board and allow them to rest for about 10 minutes.

4   **Meanwhile, make the chimichurri pesto.** In a food processor, combine the shallot, parsley, basil, Parm, pine nuts, olive oil, red wine vinegar, and garlic. Pulse until combined, then process until the sauce reaches your desired consistency (I like mine a little chunky). Taste the sauce and season with salt, black pepper, and red pepper flakes (if using) to your liking.

5   Thinly slice the steaks against the grain and serve with a generous dollop of the pesto chimichurri sauce.

We want tough cooks, not tough steaks. Remember, you can always cook a steak more, so pull it a little sooner than you think you need to. Its internal temp will rise another few degrees while it's resting.

Persian Pan Kabobs

Living in apartments for the past decade of my life has both limited me and forced me to get creative when it comes to grilling things. But, as they say, where there's a will, there's a way, and when it comes to making a kabob, my will is strong. Typically, Persian kabob koobideh is seasoned ground meat shaped around a flat metal spear and rotated over hot coals. You may not be able to achieve full smokiness without the, well, smoke, but this recipe is an easy way to get your kabob fix in the great indoors.

SERVES 4

1 small yellow onion, finely grated

1 pound ground beef (I like 80/20 grass-fed)

2 garlic cloves, minced or grated

1 teaspoon ground turmeric

1 teaspoon kosher salt

½ teaspoon freshly ground black pepper

1 tablespoon extra-virgin olive oil

For Serving

Pita or lavash

Fresh herb sprigs, such as parsley, dill, mint, and cilantro

Thickly sliced tomato

Thinly sliced red or yellow onion

Chopped cucumber

Labneh

1   One handful at a time, put the onion in a clean kitchen towel and twist and squeeze the towel over the sink to remove as much liquid as possible, then place the onion in a large bowl. Add the ground beef, garlic, turmeric, salt, and pepper to the bowl and use your hands to mix well.

2   Coat the bottom of a medium skillet with the olive oil and use a spatula or your hands to lightly spread the beef mixture evenly in the pan (don't press too hard!). Use the spatula to divide the mixture into 8 long, 1-inch-wide strips; be sure none of the kabobs are sticking to each other.

3   Cook over medium heat until the beef begins to sizzle, then cover and cook until the meat begins to release its juices (if there's quite a bit of liquid, carefully pour some off so the meat is frying, not boiling), about 4 minutes. Uncover and cook until the liquid has evaporated and the meat is sizzling, 8 to 10 minutes more. Flip the kabobs and cook until browned, 5 minutes. Remove from the heat.

4   To serve, place each kabob in a flatbread and top with fresh herbs, tomato, onion, cucumber, and labneh.

Pop the beef mixture in the fridge for 10 to 15 minutes before cooking. When ground meat is cold, it's easier to handle and shape.

Disappearing Bolognese

This recipe got its name because it has a unique way of disappearing from the pot. I like to make it on a lazy Sunday afternoon at home, and every time I do, I think, *Great, I'll have dinner covered for the week.* And every time, without fail, it's all gone two days later. But trust me, that's a good thing. You can eat this Bolognese with your favorite pasta, obviously, or you can get creative and eat it with veggies, with a crusty loaf of bread—heck, you can even eat it by itself! Whatever you do, just don't forget the freshly grated Parm.

SERVES 4

1 medium yellow onion, coarsely chopped

2 medium carrots, coarsely chopped

2 celery stalks, coarsely chopped

4 tablespoons extra-virgin olive oil

1 pound ground beef (I like 80/20 grass-fed)

Kosher salt and freshly ground black pepper

3 garlic cloves, minced or grated

1 cup dry white wine (I like sauvignon blanc)

½ cup tomato paste

1 bay leaf

¼ teaspoon ground cinnamon

Pinch of ground or freshly grated nutmeg

2 cups low-sodium chicken stock, plus more as needed

1 cup whole milk

This dish may disappear fast, but be sure to cook it slow. They say time heals all wounds—I say it makes better Bolognese.

1   In a food processor, combine the onion, carrots, and celery and pulse until very finely chopped. (Alternatively, chop the vegetables as finely as possible by hand.)

2   Heat 2 tablespoons of the olive oil in a large pot over medium heat. When the oil is shimmering, add the ground beef and season generously with salt and pepper. Cook, breaking it up with a wooden spoon, until mostly browned (it's okay if there's a little pink left), 6 to 10 minutes. Use a slotted spoon to transfer the beef to a bowl. Wipe out the pot.

3   Return the pot to medium heat and add the remaining 2 tablespoons olive oil. When the oil is shimmering, add the chopped vegetables and cook, stirring occasionally, until soft, 5 to 7 minutes. Add the garlic and cook until fragrant, 1 minute. Return the beef and any collected juices to the pot and pour in the wine. Reduce the heat to medium-low and cook, stirring occasionally, until the alcohol cooks off, about 5 minutes (you should be able to smell the difference). The beef should be finely crumbled; break up any bigger chunks.

4   Add the tomato paste, bay leaf, cinnamon, and nutmeg. Cook, stirring often, until your kitchen smells like an Italian restaurant, about 5 minutes. Pour in the stock and milk and season with salt and pepper. Reduce the heat to low and cook, uncovered, stirring from time to time, until the sauce is thick, rich, and creamy, about 3 hours; reduce the heat if it's bubbling too much. If the sauce seems too dry, add a little more stock.

5   Discard the bay leaf, taste, and season with salt and pepper to your liking. Enjoy right away, or let cool and store in an airtight container in the refrigerator for up to 1 week or in the freezer for up to 1 month.

Cola-Glazed Meatloaf

Justice for meatloaf! Such an unappetizing name for such an appetizing dish. This recipe is sizzle meets fizzle, with a cola glaze that adds unique sweetness and depth. To keep it on the leaner side and reduce greasiness, I use lean ground beef, which helps the meatloaf hold its shape. But if you're cool with a little more fat, go ahead and use the standard 80/20—just be sure to drain off the excess fat after cooking. Either way, breadcrumbs and milk will keep things moist, alongside plenty of herbs, spices, and of course that cola to bring the flavor. So grab your pan and pop a can.

SERVES 6

Meatloaf

Nonstick cooking spray

2 pounds lean ground beef (the leanest you can find; I like 94/6 grass-fed)

1 cup panko breadcrumbs

1 medium yellow onion, diced

½ cup whole milk

2 large eggs, beaten

2 garlic cloves, minced or grated

1 tablespoon finely chopped fresh parsley

1 teaspoon dried thyme

1 teaspoon dried oregano

1 teaspoon kosher salt

½ teaspoon freshly ground black pepper

½ teaspoon cayenne pepper

½ teaspoon smoked paprika

Glaze

½ cup ketchup

¼ cup Coca-Cola

2 tablespoons packed light or dark brown sugar

1 tablespoon Worcestershire sauce

2 teaspoons Dijon mustard

½ teaspoon apple cider vinegar

¼ teaspoon garlic powder

⅛ teaspoon onion powder

1 Make the meatloaf. Preheat the oven to 350°F. Line a baking sheet with aluminum foil and coat the foil with cooking spray.

2 In a large bowl, combine the ground beef, panko, onion, milk, eggs, garlic, parsley, thyme, oregano, salt, black pepper, cayenne, and paprika. Use your hands to mix until just combined. Transfer the mixture to the prepared pan, shaping it into a loaf about 9 inches long and 5 inches wide, lightly pressing to remove any air pockets.

3 Make the glaze. In a small bowl, whisk together the ketchup, Coca-Cola, brown sugar, Worcestershire, Dijon, vinegar, garlic powder, and onion powder to combine well.

4 Pour about half the glaze over the top of the meatloaf, spreading it evenly to coat. Bake the meatloaf for 45 minutes, then pour the remaining glaze over the top, rotate the pan, and bake for 15 to 20 minutes more, until the meatloaf is cooked through and has reached an internal temperature of 165°F and the glaze is caramelized. (If the glaze isn't bubbling at all, switch the oven to broil when the meatloaf reaches 160°F and broil for a few minutes to finish the glaze without overcooking the meat.)

5 Let the meatloaf rest for 5 to 10 minutes before slicing and serving.

You want your meatloaf mixture to be moist enough to, well, stay moist, but not so wet that it falls apart. If you need to adjust by adding a bit more panko or a bit more milk, feel free to make that call.

Wine-Drunk Short Ribs

My favorite kind of drunk is wine drunk. This recipe is an homage to my personal drink of choice, red wine, and the many wine hangovers I've had to nurse over the past decade. Full of body, elegance, and a bit of sass, these slow-cooked short ribs bathe in the velvety richness of red wine, allowing its deep, nuanced flavors to permeate every fiber of the tender meat. It makes for some juicy short ribs, literally. And don't worry, we're using the whole bottle, because does anyone ever really stop at one glass?

SERVES 6

1 (750ml) bottle red wine (I like cabernet sauvignon or merlot)

½ cup low-sodium soy sauce

¼ cup packed light or dark brown sugar

1 medium yellow onion, chopped

2 medium carrots, chopped

2 celery stalks, chopped

4 garlic cloves, smashed

2 sprigs rosemary

10 sprigs thyme

2 bay leaves

1 teaspoon whole black peppercorns

4 pounds beef short ribs

2 tablespoons extra-virgin olive oil

Kosher salt and freshly ground black pepper

2 tablespoons all-purpose flour

2 to 4 cups low-sodium beef stock, plus more as needed

Mash & Cheese (page 213), for serving (optional, but not really)

HOT TIP

Short ribs bring the fat, and while they cook, that fat rises right to the top of the braising liquid. Skim it off, or you'll be left with a grease feast.

1   In a large bowl, combine the wine, soy sauce, brown sugar, onion, carrots, celery, garlic, rosemary, thyme, bay leaves, and peppercorns. Arrange the short ribs in an even layer in a shallow dish. Pour over the marinade and cover the dish with plastic wrap. Marinate in the refrigerator for at least 6 hours or up to overnight, turning the ribs occasionally.

2   Preheat the oven to 325°F.

3   Heat the olive oil in a large Dutch oven or oven-safe heavy-bottomed pot over medium-high heat. Remove the ribs from the marinade (reserving the marinade) and pat them dry with paper towels. Season the ribs generously with salt and pepper. When the oil is shimmering, working in batches, add the ribs and cook, turning, until nicely browned on all sides, 10 to 12 minutes total. Transfer to a plate and repeat with the remaining ribs.

4   Sprinkle the flour into the pot (don't wipe it out) and cook, stirring continuously, until a paste forms, 1 to 2 minutes. Gradually pour in the reserved marinade, stirring and scraping up any browned bits from the bottom of the pot. Bring to a simmer. Return the ribs and any collected juices to the pot, nestling them into the liquid. If the liquid does not cover the ribs, add stock as needed to ensure they are just submerged.

5   Cover the pot and transfer to the oven. Cook for 2½ to 3 hours, until the meat is tender and easily pulls away from the bone. Remove the pot from the oven and carefully transfer the ribs to a serving platter. Use a ladle or large spoon to carefully skim the fat off the top of the braising liquid (see Hot Tip). Strain the liquid into a large bowl, discarding the solids, then pour it back into the Dutch oven. Simmer over medium heat until it thickens to your desired consistency; I usually let mine go for about 15 minutes, so it gets just a little saucy.

6   Serve the drunken short ribs with the reduced braising liquid spooned over the top and Mash & Cheese alongside, if desired (it is).

Herby Pork Larb Lettuce Wraps

Larb, a traditional Laotian dish, is said to be associated with good luck and fortune. While I can't confirm whether that's true, it does perfectly describe the way I feel while eating it: Lucky to source most of my daily joy through eating delicious food. Lucky to have the honor of learning about other cultures through their cuisines. Lucky to get to share that love and knowledge with you and the world. These refreshing wraps are packed with aromatic herbs and perfectly seasoned pork. They are somehow both light and satisfying, and I think they'll leave you feeling pretty lucky, too. You'll need a mortar and pestle or spice grinder— but if you don't have either, a food processor will work, too.

SERVES 4

¼ cup uncooked sticky rice, jasmine rice, or sushi rice

1 tablespoon vegetable oil

½ cup finely chopped shallots (about 2 medium)

3 garlic cloves, minced or grated

1 tablespoon minced fresh ginger

1 pound ground pork

1 or 2 fresh bird's-eye chiles, seeded, if desired (see Hot Tip), and finely chopped

Juice of ½ lime, plus more if needed

1 tablespoon fish sauce

1 teaspoon sugar

Kosher salt

For Serving

Large sturdy lettuce leaves or cabbage leaves

Loads of fresh herbs, such as cilantro, mint, and Thai basil

Sliced English or Persian cucumbers

Chopped roasted peanuts

Lime wedges

1   In a large skillet, toast the rice over medium heat, stirring continuously, until golden brown, 8 to 10 minutes. Transfer to a plate and let cool completely, about 30 minutes. Grind the toasted rice into a fine powder using a mortar and pestle or a spice grinder.

2   Heat the vegetable oil in the same skillet over medium-high heat. When the oil is shimmering, add the shallots and cook, stirring frequently, until translucent, 2 to 3 minutes. Add the garlic and ginger and cook, stirring often, until fragrant, about 1 minute more. Add the pork and cook, breaking it up with a wooden spoon, until cooked through and nicely browned, 7 to 10 minutes. Stir in the chiles.

3   Reduce the heat to medium and stir in the lime juice, fish sauce, and sugar. Taste and add more lime juice if you like. Remove the skillet from the heat and stir in the toasted rice powder. Taste and season with salt to your liking.

4   Lay out the pork mixture, lettuce leaves, herbs, cucumber, peanuts, and lime wedges on the table and let everyone assemble their own lettuce wraps.

Most of a chile's heat lives in its seeds and membranes, so take out some or all for a milder vibe. Practice safe spice—wash your hands after handling, and for the love of flavor, don't touch your face or eyes! Or use red pepper flakes or hot sauce!

Sausage Fest Rigatoni Bake

I used to be a festival girlie, but as my age has gone up, my tolerance for crowds and dust has gone down. I've since traded in the flower crown for an apron, because I've learned that blasting music from my kitchen is equally—if not more—enjoyable. The headliners at this festival are savory sausage, a confetti of vibrant veggies, and crowd-pleasing rigatoni, all baked to perfection with a crispy exterior and a gooey, cheesy interior. I can confidently say this is the only sausage fest you'll find in my house, and I wouldn't have it any other way.

SERVES 6 TO 10

Kosher salt and freshly ground black pepper

1 pound rigatoni

2 tablespoons extra virgin olive oil

1 pound sweet or hot Italian sausage, casings removed

1 medium yellow or red onion, finely diced

3 garlic cloves, minced or grated

1 red bell pepper, diced

1 yellow bell pepper, diced

1 medium zucchini, diced

1 (28-ounce) can crushed tomatoes

1 teaspoon dried oregano

1 teaspoon dried basil

½ teaspoon red pepper flakes

½ cup heavy cream

2 cups freshly grated mozzarella cheese

½ cup freshly grated Parmigiano Reggiano cheese

Fresh basil leaves, for serving

A mushy sausage fest is a thing of nightmares. Keep your pasta extra al dente so it can finish cooking in the sauce while it's in the oven.

1 Preheat the oven to 375°F.

2 Bring a large pot of water to a boil over high heat. Salt the water so it's salty like the tears of happiness you will cry when you taste this pasta. Add the pasta and cook until it's slightly undercooked, 3 to 4 minutes less than the package directions for al dente. Reserve 1 cup of the pasta cooking water, then drain the pasta. Transfer it to a large bowl and toss with 1 tablespoon of the olive oil.

3 Meanwhile, heat the remaining 1 tablespoon olive oil in a large skillet over medium heat. When the oil is shimmering, add the sausage and cook, breaking it up with a wooden spoon, until browned and cooked through, about 8 minutes. Use a slotted spoon to transfer the sausage to a plate.

4 Pour off all but 1 tablespoon of the fat from the pan, then return the skillet to medium heat. Add the onion and cook, stirring frequently, until soft and translucent, about 5 minutes. Add the garlic and cook until fragrant, 1 minute. Add the red and yellow bell peppers and the zucchini and season with salt and black pepper. Cook, stirring occasionally, until the vegetables are slightly softened, about 5 minutes more.

5 Return the sausage and any collected juices to the skillet. Pour in the crushed tomatoes and about half the reserved pasta cooking water. Stir in the oregano, dried basil, and red pepper flakes. Bring the sauce to a simmer, cover, and cook, stirring once or twice, until the flavors have melded, 15 to 20 minutes. Stir in the cream. Taste and season with salt and black pepper to your liking.

6 Add the cooked pasta to the pan and toss to coat evenly with the sauce; if it's too thick, add another splash of the pasta cooking water. Transfer half the saucy rigatoni mixture to a large baking dish. Sprinkle on half the mozzarella and half the Parm. Layer the remaining saucy rigatoni over the cheese and top with the remaining cheeses.

7 Bake the rigatoni for 20 to 25 minutes, until the cheese is melted and bubbling. Remove from the oven and let stand for 10 minutes. Garnish with fresh basil and serve.

EIGHT

SIDES

Mash & Cheese

I knew I wanted to create a unique recipe for mashed potatoes, and *boy*, was it a roller coaster. I went through so many ideas and iterations, but nothing was sticking—or should I say spudding. While making mac and cheese one Sunday afternoon, I started playing around with a wild idea: What if I made mashed potatoes like I make mac and cheese? (This is what counts as *wild* after age 30.) Well, it WORKED, and this dish was born. We're making the cheesiest cheese sauce and incorporating it into the potatoes to make for the dreamiest mash. It's a mash made in heaven.

Serves 4 to 6

6 large potatoes (about 2½ pounds total; I like half Yukon Golds and half russets), peeled and cut into 1-inch cubes

Kosher salt

4 tablespoons (½ stick) unsalted butter

2 tablespoons all-purpose flour

½ teaspoon mustard powder

1 cup whole milk

1½ cups freshly grated sharp cheddar cheese

1 cup freshly grated Gruyère cheese

Panko breadcrumbs (optional)

1 tablespoon unsalted butter, melted (optional)

Finely chopped fresh chives, for serving

1   Place the potatoes in a large pot and add water to cover. Salt the water so it's salty like the tears of happiness you will cry when you eat this mash. Bring to a boil over medium-high heat, then cook until the potatoes are fork-tender, 12 to 15 minutes.

2   Meanwhile, melt the butter in a medium saucepan over medium heat. Add the flour and mustard powder and cook, whisking continuously, until a roux forms, 2 to 3 minutes. It should be thick and bubbling. Gradually whisk in the milk until the mixture thickens into a smooth sauce. Reduce the heat to low and slowly add the cheddar and Gruyère, stirring until fully melted. Taste and season with salt to your liking.

3   Drain the potatoes, return them to their pot, and use a potato masher or fork to mash them to your preferred texture. While slowly mixing with a wooden spoon, pour in the cheese sauce and stir just until well combined. Taste and adjust the seasoning to your liking.

4   Optional but highly recommended: Preheat the broiler. Transfer the mash to an 8-cup baking dish, sprinkle the top evenly with panko, and drizzle with the melted butter. Broil for a few minutes, until a golden crust forms. The timing will depend on your broiler, so watch the whole time to keep the panko from burning.

5   Sprinkle with chives and serve!

Cheese solidifies as it cools, so if you make your mash ahead of time, keep the mashed potatoes and the cheese sauce separate. When you're ready to serve, reheat both components and *then* mix them together.

Broccolini
WITH SPICY PEANUT SAUCE

I love peanut sauce so much I could happily eat Styrofoam smothered in it. Luckily, we have plenty of actual foods to pour it on, so I don't need to do that. You know how parents hide vegetables in some dishes to trick their kids into eating them? Well, this is kind of that. Being that I am a big kid at heart, sometimes I smother my broccoli in peanut sauce to trick myself into eating my veggies. I personally love the long, tender stems and small florets of broccolini, but regular broccoli works well here.

Serves 4

1 pound (about 2 bunches) broccolini, ends trimmed

¼ cup extra-virgin olive oil

Kosher salt and freshly ground black pepper

¼ cup any creamy peanut butter

2 tablespoons low-sodium soy sauce

2 tablespoons rice vinegar

1 tablespoon honey

1 tablespoon toasted sesame oil

1 tablespoon sambal oelek or sriracha

1 garlic clove, minced or grated

¼ cup chopped roasted peanuts, for serving (optional)

1   Preheat the oven to 425°F.

2   In a large bowl, toss the broccolini with the olive oil and season with salt and pepper. Arrange in a single layer on a baking sheet. Roast the broccolini for about 20 minutes, flipping them after 15 minutes, until tender and slightly charred.

3   Meanwhile, in a small bowl, whisk together the peanut butter, soy sauce, vinegar, honey, sesame oil, sambal oelek, garlic, and 2 tablespoons water until smooth.

4   Transfer the roasted broccolini to a serving dish and drizzle with the spicy peanut sauce. Sprinkle the chopped peanuts over the top, if desired, and enjoy!

Don't foil your fun—foil your baking sheet for easy cleanup. It means less scrubbing and more grubbing.

Persian Salad Shirazi

As I was falling in love with Zoya, I was also falling in love with Persian cuisine. There is so much to learn about Persian culture; for me, food was an easy and natural first step—and it led to so much more than a meal. Cooking these dishes deepened my relationship with Zoya, helped me bond with her family (including her Farsi-speaking extended relatives!), and brought me closer to my ever-growing Persian community. I just couldn't leave this recipe out of my first book because this zesty, refreshing side salad has a special place in my heart. I love an heirloom when in season, hence those lovely yellow tomatoes, but use whatever you have on hand. It's fresh, juicy, and the perfect companion, just like Zoya.

Serves 4 to 6

2 ripe large tomatoes, diced

1 small red onion, finely diced

2 Persian cucumbers, diced

2 teaspoons dried mint (optional)

Juice of ½ lemon

2 tablespoons extra-virgin olive oil

Kosher salt

1   In a medium bowl, stir together the tomatoes, onion, cucumbers, mint (if using), and lemon juice. Drizzle with the olive oil and season with salt. Toss gently to coat evenly. Taste and adjust the seasoning to your liking.

2   Serve right away and enjoy!

Cutting tomatoes is the ultimate test of a good knife—a dull one will crush the tomato instead of slicing it. A serrated knife works best, if you have one.

Chop Slaw

It's like coleslaw, but finer—as fine as you. Okay, maybe not *that* fine, but you get the idea. A good slaw recipe is like a good pair of jeans: Dress 'em up, dress 'em down, hit a picnic or the town. Did I just write a poem? Call it slam poetry—or should I say *slaw* poetry. This one is crunchy and tangy, but don't get too caught up with amounts here—this is a good low-stakes recipe to experiment with ingredients and flavors. The name of the game is just chopping it all into small, even bits. To me, that makes it fun to eat. Slap it on a sandwich (like the Veggie Joes on page 115), on a chip, or even on the table as a salad.

1   In a large bowl, combine the green cabbage, purple cabbage, carrots, cilantro, and scallions.

2   In a small bowl, whisk together the mayonnaise, vinegar, Dijon, and honey and season with salt and pepper. Taste and adjust the seasoning to your liking.

3   Pour the dressing over the slaw mixture. Using tongs or two spoons, toss to coat well. Cover the bowl with plastic wrap and refrigerate for at least 30 minutes or up to overnight.

4   When ready to serve, sprinkle on the slivered almonds and crispy fried onions and toss again to combine.

Serves 4 to 6

1 cup finely chopped green cabbage

1 cup finely chopped purple cabbage

2 large carrots, grated or cut into thin matchsticks

½ cup fresh cilantro, finely chopped

½ cup sliced scallions

¼ cup mayonnaise

1½ tablespoons apple cider vinegar

1 tablespoon Dijon mustard

1 tablespoon honey

Kosher salt and freshly ground black pepper

1 cup slivered almonds, toasted

½ cup crispy fried onions, store-bought or homemade (see page 234)

CHOP CHOP! But actually, take your time. You've got a lot of chopping to do, so protect your fingers and don't move too quickly.

Flash-Fried Garlicky Snap Peas

SNAPS FOR SNAP PEAS! Snap peas are such an underutilized vegetable, and it's a shame because they are one of my favorites. They are bursting with sweetness and an incredible crunch that stands up to heat when cooked (but not for too long). This dish is my personal favorite way to make them. Flash-frying preserves that SNAP and color, and the sesame-soy sauce is simple and satisfying.

Serves 4

2 tablespoons vegetable oil

1 pound snap peas, trimmed

4 garlic cloves, thinly sliced

1 tablespoon low-sodium soy sauce

1 teaspoon toasted sesame oil

½ teaspoon red pepper flakes

Kosher salt and freshly ground black pepper

Toasted sesame seeds, for serving

Sliced scallions, for serving

1   Heat the vegetable oil in a large skillet or wok over high heat. When the oil is shimmering, add the snap peas and cook, stirring continuously, until the peas are bright green and slightly tender but still crisp, 1 to 2 minutes. Reduce the heat to medium and add the garlic. Cook, stirring, until fragrant, 30 seconds to 1 minute.

2   Drizzle in the soy sauce and sesame oil and add the red pepper flakes. Toss to coat the snap peas evenly. Season with salt and black pepper.

3   Transfer the snap peas to a serving dish. Sprinkle with sesame seeds and scallions. Serve immediately and enjoy!

If you're in a pinch (or better yet, a snap), you can easily swap the snap peas out for green beans.

Heirloom Tomato & Potato Salad
WITH HOT HONEY VINAIGRETTE

You may already know about my enthusiasm for ABL (anything but lettuce) salads—though I can get behind the occasional lettuce leaf. And if the salad involves carbs? Immediately sold. Potato salad is giving . . . potluck. Let's be honest—it desperately needs a rebrand. So I took on the role of publicist: Consider this recipe potato salad's glow-up. I like to use yellow Dutch potatoes, for their buttery flavor, but the multicolored ones are fun, too. To elevate things, I've added heirloom tomatoes for some sophistication, color, acid, and juiciness. Everything gets dressed up in a hot honey vinaigrette that's dripping with spicy sex appeal. This is the potato salad makeover of the generation.

Serves 4 to 6

Kosher salt

1½ pounds baby potatoes, halved or quartered

3 tablespoons extra-virgin olive oil

2 tablespoons apple cider vinegar

2 tablespoons Dijon mustard

2 tablespoons hot honey

Freshly ground black pepper

1 shallot, thinly sliced

2 garlic cloves, thinly sliced

1½ pounds heirloom tomatoes, cut the same size as the potatoes

Finely chopped fresh dill

Flaky salt, for serving

1   Bring a large pot of water to a boil over medium-high heat. Salt the water so it's salty like the tears of happiness you will cry when you eat this salad. Add the potatoes and cook until tender when pierced with a fork, 10 to 15 minutes.

2   Meanwhile, in a large bowl, whisk together 2 tablespoons of the olive oil, the vinegar, mustard, and hot honey until well combined. Taste and season with salt and pepper to your liking.

3   Drain the potatoes, immediately add them to the bowl with the dressing, and toss to coat.

4   In a small skillet, combine the remaining 1 tablespoon olive oil, the shallot, and garlic. Cook over medium-low heat, stirring, until soft and fragrant, about 4 minutes. Add the garlic-shallot mixture to the potatoes and stir to combine. Cover the bowl and refrigerate for at least 30 minutes or up to overnight before serving.

5   Just before serving, add the tomatoes and as much dill as your heart desires, and gently toss. Taste and adjust the seasoning to your liking. Transfer to a serving dish, sprinkle with flaky salt, and enjoy!

Be sure to cut all the potatoes, even the itty-bitty ones! Whole potatoes won't absorb the dressing.

Creamed Corn

My second grade teacher tasked us with submitting our favorite Thanksgiving recipes for a class cookbook. As the budding home cook I already was, I submitted my family's apple chestnut stuffing recipe (saving that one for the next book). When our class cookbook was distributed to us, I flipped through, only to discover my recipe had been left out. My face swollen from tears, I found a Sharpie and went to town on the front cover to express my anger. My parents think this might have been the catalyst for my entire career, which I can neither confirm nor deny. We still have that cookbook and pull it out every year, not just as a (now hilarious) reminder of my childhood trauma, but also for *this* one recipe. It's evolved into our own over the years, and everyone who tries it asks for it. It's so simple but so good—dare I say I would go through the entire traumatic experience again to have this recipe.

1   In a large saucepan, combine the corn, cream, milk, and sugar and season with salt and the cayenne. Bring to a boil over medium heat, stirring occasionally, then reduce the heat to low and simmer until the corn is heated through, about 5 minutes.

2   In a small bowl, whisk together the melted butter and the flour, then add the mixture to the corn. Cook, stirring often, until the liquid thickens, about 3 minutes. To test the thickness, dip a wooden spoon in the creamed corn and slide your finger through it—it should leave a trail. If it doesn't, cook for another minute and check again. Taste and add more salt and cayenne to your liking. Remove from the heat and transfer to a serving bowl.

3   Sprinkle with the chives and serve hot!

Serves 6

1 (16-ounce) bag frozen sweet corn kernels

1 cup heavy cream

1 cup whole milk

2 tablespoons sugar

Kosher salt

Pinch of cayenne pepper, plus more as needed

2 tablespoons unsalted butter, melted

2 tablespoons all-purpose flour

Chopped fresh chives, for serving

One year my mom mistakenly added two tablespoons of salt instead of sugar, so don't do that.

Spicy Honey Roasted Carrots
WITH RICOTTA & PISTACHIOS

Zoya is an incredible cook—she's even more skilled than I am (but don't tell her I admitted that). One thing she stands by is that vegetables, if prepared with creativity and love, are way more impressive than meat. This recipe is a play on one of Zoya's signature vegetable dishes that might just prove her point. While simple, these roasted carrots are sophisticated and sexy. With creaminess and crunch, sweetness and spice, this side dish is no sidepiece.

Serves 4

2 tablespoons honey, plus more for drizzling

1 tablespoon extra-virgin olive oil

1 tablespoon unsalted butter, melted

½ teaspoon red pepper flakes

½ teaspoon ground sumac

Kosher salt and freshly ground black pepper

1 pound small rainbow carrots, trimmed and halved lengthwise

½ cup full-fat ricotta cheese

¼ cup fresh dill, finely chopped

Zest of ½ lemon (optional)

Juice of ½ lemon (optional)

¼ cup roasted salted pistachios or toasted shelled raw pistachios, coarsely chopped

Flaky salt, for serving

1 Preheat the oven to 400°F. Line a baking sheet with parchment paper.

2 In a large bowl, whisk together the honey, olive oil, melted butter, red pepper flakes, and sumac and season with salt and black pepper. Taste and adjust the seasoning to your liking. Add the carrots and toss to coat evenly.

3 Arrange the carrots in a single layer on the prepared baking sheet. Roast the carrots for 20 to 25 minutes, flipping halfway through, until tender and caramelized around the edges.

4 Meanwhile, in a small bowl, stir together the ricotta and dill. Season with salt and black pepper and mix to combine. Assess your ricotta—if it's thin, pour off any liquid, add the lemon zest, and stir well; if it's thick, stir in the lemon juice. Taste and adjust the seasoning to your liking.

5 Smear the ricotta mixture over the bottom of a serving dish. Arrange the roasted carrots on top of the ricotta. Drizzle the carrots with a little more honey and sprinkle with the pistachios and some flaky salt before serving.

We're caramelizing the carrots, and this process moves fast. The honey can burn if you're not careful, so keep a watchful eye and check periodically while roasting.

Miso-Glazed Eggplant

Some ingredients just instantly intimidate. Two that make the list for me are miso and eggplant. My rule of thumb, for cooking and life, is: The more intimidating something is, the simpler you go. Miso's savory depth and eggplant's silky charm make this simply cooked side a fantastic addition to your repertoire of vegetable dishes. I think you'll find these objects are friendlier (and even tastier) than they appear.

Serves 4

2 medium or 4 small Japanese or Chinese eggplants (12 ounces total), stems trimmed

2 tablespoons white miso paste

2 tablespoons mirin (sweet rice wine)

1 tablespoon low-sodium soy sauce

1 tablespoon rice vinegar

1 tablespoon sugar

1 tablespoon vegetable oil

1 tablespoon toasted sesame oil

2 garlic cloves, minced or grated

1 teaspoon grated fresh ginger

Toasted sesame seeds, for serving

Sliced scallions, for serving

1   Preheat the oven to 400°F.

2   Cut the eggplants in half lengthwise, then make diagonal cuts into the flesh about an inch apart, creating a crisscross pattern without cutting all the way through to the skin.

3   In a small bowl, whisk together the miso, mirin, soy sauce, vinegar, and sugar until smooth. Brush the cut sides of the eggplants with the miso glaze, being sure to get it into the crevices you made. Set aside to marinate at room temperature for 10 to 15 minutes.

4   Heat the vegetable oil in a large oven-safe skillet over medium-high heat. When the oil is shimmering, add the eggplant halves, cut-side down. Cook, undisturbed, until nicely browned on the bottom, 2 to 3 minutes. Flip the eggplant, brush the cut sides with any remaining glaze, and transfer the skillet to the oven.

5   Bake for 10 to 15 minutes, until the eggplant is tender when pierced with a fork and the glaze is caramelized.

6   Meanwhile, in a small saucepan, combine the sesame oil, garlic, and ginger. Cook over medium heat, stirring continuously, until fragrant, about 3 minutes.

7   Remove the eggplant from the oven and drizzle the sesame oil mixture over them. Sprinkle with sesame seeds and scallions and serve hot.

Cutting the crisscross pattern into the eggplant isn't just for looks; it maximizes glaze absorption and ensures an even cook

Crispy Smashed Potatoes au Gratin

I didn't think it was possible for au gratin to be any better than it already is. It's a staple recipe on our holiday table—and I mean every holiday table, because we love it that much. Au gratin is, in fact, my favorite of all potato preparations, of which there are many. I knew I couldn't make a better version of something that's already perfect, so instead, let's just call this recipe "different." What's different here is that I've replaced the potato slices with smashed potatoes, which adds crispy bits to enhance the creamy ones. Not better, just different.

Serves 6

Unsalted butter, for greasing

1½ pounds baby potatoes (I like Dutch potatoes)

Kosher salt

1½ cups heavy cream

3 tablespoons unsalted butter, melted

2 garlic cloves, minced or grated

Freshly ground black pepper

2 cups freshly grated Gruyère cheese

½ cup freshly grated Parmigiano Reggiano cheese

Finely chopped fresh thyme leaves or parsley, for serving

Don't get too smashed or your potatoes may fall apart.

1   Preheat the oven to 350°F. Grease a 9 × 12-inch baking dish with butter.

2   Place the potatoes in a large pot and add water to cover. Salt the water so it's salty like the tears of happiness you will cry when you taste this gratin. Cook over medium-high heat until the potatoes are fork-tender, about 40 minutes total, but check on smaller ones earlier. Drain the potatoes, scatter them over a cutting board, and let stand until they are cool enough to handle.

3   Using a fork or the bottom of a drinking glass, gently smash the potatoes down to flatten them to about ½ inch thick, keeping them intact.

4   In a liquid measuring cup, stir together the cream, melted butter, and garlic. Season with salt and pepper.

5   Arrange half the smashed potatoes in a single layer in the prepared baking dish. Pour over half the cream mixture, season with salt and pepper, and top with half the Gruyère. Add the remaining potatoes, the remaining cream mixture, then the remaining Gruyère.

6   Bake for 25 to 30 minutes, until the cream is reduced and bubbling. Switch the oven to broil and cook for 2 to 3 minutes more, until the top is golden and crispy.

7   Remove from the oven and immediately top with the Parm. Sprinkle with thyme and enjoy straight from the baking dish!

Saucy Noods

Have you ever made saucy noods? Get your mind out of the gutter and into the kitchen, because these will have you sending noods to all your friends. This recipe is kind of like Mary Poppins's bag: a small package that just keeps on giving. It's simple, but somehow contains anything you might ever want or need. It's salty, sweet, saucy, and—best of all—extra garlicky. (I was going to name them garlic noods, but you know the deal with noods: the saucier, the better.)

Serves 4

Kosher salt

8 ounces noodles of your choice

2 tablespoons oyster sauce

1 tablespoon low-sodium soy sauce

1 tablespoon light brown sugar

1 teaspoon toasted sesame oil

4 tablespoons (½ stick) unsalted butter

6 to 8 garlic cloves, minced or grated

2 scallions, thinly sliced, plus more for serving

¼ cup freshly grated Parmigiano Reggiano cheese

Toasted sesame seeds, for serving

1 Bring a large pot of water to a boil over high heat. Salt the water so it's salty like the tears of happiness you will cry when you eat these noodles. Add the noodles and cook until al dente according to the package directions. Reserve ½ cup of the noodle cooking water, then drain the noodles.

2 Meanwhile, in a small bowl, whisk together the oyster sauce, soy sauce, brown sugar, and sesame oil.

3 Melt the butter in a large skillet over medium-high heat. Add the garlic and cook, stirring often, until golden, 2 to 3 minutes. Pour in the oyster sauce mixture and stir to combine. Add the scallions, then add the cooked noodles and Parm and toss until the noodles are well coated and the sauce looks glossy. Splash in some of the reserved noodle cooking water if the noodles look too dry.

4 Divide the noods among four bowls. Garnish with more scallions and sesame seeds. Enjoy right away!

Never share saucy noods—keep them all for yourself.

Leeky Mac & Cheese
WITH CRISPY FRIED ONION CRUMBS

I have a hot take: Mac and cheese is delicious, but it's just begging for a little extra something. Enter leeks—pungent yet subtle, they bring a delicate sweetness and savoriness that elevates the whole dish. It's proof that even the simplest things have room for depth. And speaking of depth, why settle for regular breadcrumbs when you can have crispy fried onion crumbs? We're making those from scratch here, but if you want to go the store-bought route, grab a cup of fried onions and call it a day—no judgement!

Serves 8 to 10

2 tablespoons unsalted butter, plus more for greasing

Crispy Fried Onions

2 cups vegetable oil, for frying

½ medium yellow onion, thinly sliced

1 cup buttermilk

1 cup all-purpose flour

Kosher salt

Mac and Cheese

Kosher salt

8 ounces elbow macaroni, small shells, or orecchiette

2 medium leeks, white and light green parts only, halved lengthwise, thinly sliced, and cleaned (see Hot Tip, page 236)

3 tablespoons all-purpose flour

2½ cups whole milk

2 cups freshly grated sharp cheddar cheese

1 cup freshly grated Gruyère cheese or another favorite melting cheese, such as Fontina or Gouda

Freshly ground black pepper

2 tablespoons freshly grated Parmigiano Reggiano cheese

Finely chopped fresh parsley, for serving

1   Preheat the oven to 375°F. Grease a 9×12-inch baking dish with butter.

2   **Make the fried onions.** Pour the vegetable oil into a large deep skillet. Clip a deep-fry thermometer to the side of the pan and heat the oil over medium-high heat until it reaches 375°F (see the Hot Tip on page 79). Line a plate with paper towels.

3   In a medium bowl, combine the onion and buttermilk and set aside to soak for 10 minutes. Place 1 cup of the flour in a shallow bowl. Working in batches, lift a handful of the onions from the buttermilk, allowing the excess to drip off, and dredge them in the flour to coat, shaking off any excess flour. Add the coated onions to the hot oil and cook, stirring occasionally, until golden and crispy, 2 to 3 minutes. Use a slotted spoon to transfer to the paper towels to drain and immediately season with salt. Repeat with the remaining onions.

4   **Make the mac and cheese.** Fill a large Dutch oven or heavy-bottomed pot with water and bring to a boil over high heat. Salt the water so it's salty like the tears of happiness you will cry when you eat this mac and cheese. Add the macaroni and cook for 3 to 4 minutes less than the package directions for al dente, then drain.

5   In the pot you used for the pasta, melt the butter over medium-high heat. Add the leeks and cook, stirring occasionally, until soft and slightly caramelized, 8 to 10 minutes. Sprinkle the remaining 3 tablespoons flour over the leeks and stir to coat. Reduce the heat to low and cook, stirring continuously, until the raw flour taste has cooked out, 1 to 2 minutes.

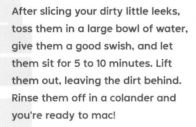

After slicing your dirty little leeks, toss them in a large bowl of water, give them a good swish, and let them sit for 5 to 10 minutes. Lift them out, leaving the dirt behind. Rinse them off in a colander and you're ready to mac!

6 Gradually pour in the milk, whisking continuously to avoid lumps. Increase the heat to medium-low and cook, stirring often, until it thickens and becomes creamy, and coats the back of a spoon (when you lift your spoon out of the sauce and draw a line down it with your finger, it leaves a trail), 5 to 7 minutes. Slowly whisk in the cheddar and Gruyère, allowing them to melt into the sauce and create a smooth mixture, 2 to 3 minutes. Remove the pot from the heat and season the cheese sauce generously with salt and pepper to your liking (it needs a good amount of salt).

7 Add the cooked macaroni to the cheese sauce and stir to coat evenly. Taste and adjust the seasoning again. Transfer the macaroni and cheese mixture to the prepared baking dish.

8 In a food processor, pulse the crispy fried onions into coarse crumbs (they may get a little soggy, but don't worry, they'll crisp up again), or place them on a cutting board and coarsely chop. Sprinkle the crispy fried onion crumbs and the Parm over the top of the mac and cheese.

9 Bake for 20 to 25 minutes, until the top is golden and crispy and the sauce is bubbling. If you like, switch the oven to broil and cook for a few minutes for an even crispier topping, watching carefully to prevent burning.

10 Remove from the oven and let cool for 10 to 15 minutes. Garnish with parsley and serve hot.

STARTING FROM SCRATCH

Remember back on page 138 when I said I was the Energizer bunny? Well, even those batteries run out of juice. Turns out burnout is very real, and after years at Tasty, it hit hard. I was regular on-camera talent in shows like *Behind Tasty* and *I Draw, You Cook*. But my job was still to make hands-only videos. I was struggling to keep up and find motivation when my body was begging me to slow down. When people ask me how to find purpose, I say look to your childhood and let fun lead the way. I had so much fun being on camera, but I was spread so thin that my spark was fading. The in-between before making a big decision is tough. Stay or go? Sit down or jump? Fall or fly? One day, during yet another conversation about video quotas, I made my decision, and put in my two weeks.

Everyone told me I was crazy; I was at the height of my career, Tasty was my golden ticket, how could I walk away? But no matter how many people told me I would fail (and many did), I knew I had to. I will always choose to bet on myself. While leaving the safety net of Tasty was scary, I trusted I would be okay. After leaving, I planned to take two weeks off from making videos, but as soon as I pressed pause, the burnout unleashed. Two weeks stretched into two months, which stretched into a year.

The feeling of having found my purpose was fleeting; many people were making cooking videos by then, and I questioned my own legitimacy. At Tasty, my home-cook skill level was my superpower; now it felt like a hindrance. I had an idea for a cookbook—this cookbook—and while publishers were reaching out, I didn't feel ready, or even confident enough, to write it.

When the pandemic hit, I felt my spark ignite. *Everyone* was stuck at home, scared, looking for connection through digital means, and—whether out of boredom or necessity—learning how to cook. If I could continue to spread some happiness through recipes, it felt like a small way I could help. I dove back into making videos, first on YouTube and then on a new platform, TikTok. On the other side of the pandemic, I had built up a social presence all my own—and with it, my confidence.

When you feel like you've figured it all out, life will throw you a curveball and you'll have to start from scratch. My life has been full of curveballs, but I'm never truly starting from scratch because the lessons I've learned along the way pave the way. We are all just one lifelong work in progress, sometimes moving two steps ahead, then two steps back, having to pivot, scratch it, or slide to the left, but always, somehow moving forward.

That brings me right back to you. *You* who have watched me make mess after mistake, and have laughed with me, learned with me, cried with me, opened your kitchens, homes, and hearts. When people see me out in the world, they often say, "I grew up watching you!" And while I can't believe I am old enough for people to say that, I feel so damn lucky to share my recipes and my life with you. While you grew up, I grew up, too. In your moments of doubt, whether in the kitchen or the world, I hope you can remember to say scratch that when things don't go as planned and just keep cooking.

SWEET

TREATS

Toasted Coconut Key Lime Pie

This recipe was born in 2020 amid the viral spread of sourdough starter and banana bread. I made it for my best friend Sydney's birthday and left it on her stoop. It's a slice of pure sunshine, bright and zingy but softened by the rich sweetness of the toasted coconut and whipped cream—the perfect representation of how sweetness and sourness can coexist beautifully. If you can find key limes, their flavor is more intense and tangy—perfect for pie. Just keep in mind that they're smaller, so you'll need more of them, and juicing them can be a time commitment. Regular limes are better than bottled juice if that's your only choice.

Makes one 9-inch pie

Crust

8 graham crackers

½ cup unsweetened shredded coconut

¼ cup macadamia nuts

4 tablespoons (½ stick) unsalted butter, melted

2 tablespoons sugar

Pinch of kosher salt

Key Lime Filling

4 large egg yolks

2 (14-ounce) cans sweetened condensed milk

¾ cup fresh key lime juice (from about 1 pound key limes)

Topping

1 cup heavy cream

1 tablespoon plus 1 teaspoon sugar

1 teaspoon pure vanilla extract

Zest of 1 key lime

Before juicing, give your citrus a little love by rolling it on the countertop with the palm of your hand. This helps loosen the juices, making it much easier to squeeze out every last drop. Trust me, the juice is worth the squeeze!

1   Make the crust. Preheat the oven to 350°F.

2   Place the graham crackers in a food processor and pulse into fine crumbs; you should have about 1¼ cups. Transfer to a medium bowl. Combine the coconut and nuts in the food processor and pulse until crushed—some bigger pieces are okay. Transfer to a small skillet. Cook over medium heat, stirring often, until golden and lightly toasted, 4 to 5 minutes. Transfer half the toasted mixture to the bowl with the graham cracker crumbs (reserve the remainder for serving). Pour in the melted butter, then add the sugar and salt and use your hands to combine well.

3   Press the crumbs over the bottom and up the sides of a 9-inch pie dish, being sure to pack them in tightly. Bake the crust for 8 to 10 minutes, until golden and set.

4   Meanwhile, make the filling. Place the egg yolks in a large bowl, add the condensed milk and lime juice, and whisk until smooth.

5   Pour the filling into the warm crust. Bake for 12 to 15 minutes, until the filling is mostly set but still slightly jiggly in the center. Remove from the oven and let cool to room temperature, then cover and refrigerate for at least 1 hour or up to 3 days before serving.

6   Just before serving, make the topping. In a large bowl, combine the cream, 1 tablespoon of the sugar, and the vanilla and whip with a handheld mixer on medium speed or by hand until soft peaks form (meaning when you stop mixing and pull out the beaters or whisk, the whipped cream forms a "mountain peak" but the top falls over), about 3 minutes, or longer by hand.

7   In a small bowl, combine the lime zest with the remaining 1 teaspoon sugar and use your fingertips to pinch them together to release the oils in the zest.

8   Spread the whipped cream over the top of the pie, then sprinkle the sugared lime zest and the reserved toasted coconut mixture over the top. Slice and enjoy!

Almond Olive Oil Cake

I grew up with an almond mom, but not the ultra-healthy kind—the Dutch kind. I'm Dutch by heritage, and though my family has grown distant from our roots, one lasting trait is our love of all things almond—we're nuts about it! I don't think almonds are officially a Dutch thing, so don't quote me on that, but sugary almond baked goods appear at all of our holidays, birthdays, weddings, and gatherings of all kinds. This cake is my nutty twist on the viral olive oil cake. I thought its moist richness would pair perfectly with the sweet, dense foundation of almond cake, and I was right! *So* right that this is now my official birthday cake.

Serves 6 to 8

Unsalted butter, for greasing

1 cup almond flour

1 cup all-purpose flour

1½ teaspoons baking powder

½ teaspoon baking soda

¼ teaspoon kosher salt

1 cup granulated sugar

3 large eggs, at room temperature

1 cup extra-virgin olive oil

1 cup whole milk, at room temperature

1 teaspoon pure vanilla extract

1 teaspoon almond extract

Zest of 1 lemon (optional)

½ cup sliced almonds

Powdered sugar, for serving

Fresh berries, for serving

1   Preheat the oven to 350°F. Grease a 9-inch round cake pan with butter and line the bottom with a round of parchment paper cut to fit.

2   In a medium bowl, stir together the almond flour, all-purpose flour, baking powder, baking soda, and salt. In a large bowl, whisk together the granulated sugar and eggs until well combined, pale, and slightly fluffy. Add the olive oil, milk, vanilla, almond extract, and lemon zest (if using). Mix until smooth. Gradually add the dry ingredients to the wet, stirring until just combined. Take care not to overmix; a few lumps are okay. Pour the batter into the prepared cake pan.

3   Bake for 20 minutes, then sprinkle the sliced almonds evenly over the top. Bake for 10 to 15 minutes more, until a toothpick inserted into the center of the cake comes out clean. Remove from the oven and let cool in the pan for about 10 minutes, then transfer the cake to a wire rack to cool completely, 1 to 2 hours.

4   Dust the cooled cake with powdered sugar (see Hot Tip, page 253). Top with berries, slice, and enjoy! This cake is best the day it's made, but it's so good, you won't have any problems finishing it, I'm sure.

Cooking is about intuition; baking is about precision. Always do the spoon and scrape method when measuring flour—spoon flour into your measuring cup and level it off by scraping with the top of a knife. Too much flour can lead to a dense cake.

Salted Malted Brown Butter Chocolate Chip Cookies

Everyone needs a go-to cookie, and this is mine. It takes everything good about a chocolate chip cookie and multiplies it: The butter is browned and salted, the milk is powdered and malted, and they somehow manage to be both perfectly chewy and crispy. I know I'm calling these chocolate chip cookies but—brace yourself—I think chocolate chip cookies are even better WITHOUT the chocolate chips. (And don't tell me that makes it a sugar cookie—sugar cookies are basic and sweet, and the base of a chocolate chip cookie is rich, buttery, and complex.) For me, the chocolate gets in the way. I know many people out there will passionately disagree with me, and I'm not one to tell you what to do, so consider this a choose-your-own-chocolate adventure.

Makes about 4 dozen cookies

1 cup (2 sticks) salted butter

2 cups all-purpose flour

1 teaspoon baking soda

¾ cup packed light brown sugar

¾ cup granulated sugar

2 large eggs, at room temperature

½ cup malted milk powder

2 teaspoons pure vanilla extract

Up to 12 ounces semisweet or milk chocolate chips (optional)

Flaky salt

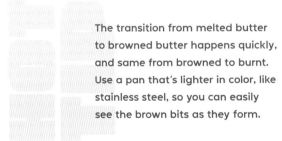

The transition from melted butter to browned butter happens quickly, and same from browned to burnt. Use a pan that's lighter in color, like stainless steel, so you can easily see the brown bits as they form.

1 Melt the butter in a small saucepan over medium heat, then cook, stirring continuously, just until brown bits appear at the bottom and the butter smells nutty and fragrant, about 7 minutes. Immediately transfer the butter to a small heatproof bowl, being sure to scrape out all the browned milk solids from the pan. Let cool for about 10 minutes.

2 In a small bowl, whisk together the flour and baking soda. In a large bowl, whisk together the brown sugar, granulated sugar, and cooled brown butter until well combined. Add the eggs and whisk until smooth. Add the malted milk powder and vanilla and whisk again. Add the dry ingredients to the wet ingredients and stir with a spatula to combine—don't overmix. Fold in as many chocolate chips as your heart desires, or skip them. Cover the bowl with plastic wrap and refrigerate for at least 1 hour or up to overnight.

3 When you're ready to bake, position a rack in the center of the oven and preheat to 375°F. Line a baking sheet with parchment paper.

4 Scoop 1-tablespoon portions of the dough onto the prepared baking sheet, leaving at least 2 inches between each. Sprinkle each cookie with a little flaky salt. (At this point, you can freeze the balls of dough on the baking sheet until solid, then transfer them to a resealable plastic bag and store in the freezer for up to 3 months. When the craving strikes, bake them straight from frozen, adding a minute or two to the baking time.)

5 Bake for 8 to 10 minutes, until the edges are golden brown. Remove from the oven. For a softer cookie, let them rest on the baking sheet for 3 minutes before transferring to a wire rack; for a crispier cookie, let them rest for 10 minutes. Either way, let them cool completely on the rack before eating, about 1 hour. Store the cookies in an airtight container at room temperature for up to a few days.

Ritzy Crisp Treats

Some people have a sweet tooth; I have a salty tooth. I love a Rice Krispies Treat, but as the grown woman I am, I was looking for a saltier, butterier version. I know it may sound odd, but the crushed Ritz crackers really play well with the sweetness of the marshmallows. Some stories are from rags to riches; mine is from rice to Ritzes.

Makes 16 treats

½ cup (1 stick) unsalted butter, plus more for greasing

3 sleeves Ritz crackers (about 96 crackers)

1 (16-ounce) bag mini marshmallows

2 teaspoons pure vanilla extract

1 Grease an 8-inch square baking dish with butter.

2 Place the crackers in a resealable plastic bag and crush into quarter-size crumbs (it's okay if there are some fine crumbs, too).

3 Melt the butter in a large saucepan over medium heat, then cook, stirring continuously, just until brown bits appear at the bottom and the butter smells nutty and fragrant, about 7 minutes. Immediately add the mini marshmallows and vanilla, remove from the heat, and stir until the marshmallows are completely melted, 2 to 3 minutes. Stir in the cracker crumbs to combine evenly.

4 Transfer the mixture to the prepared baking dish and use a spatula to spread it into an even layer. Refrigerate until firm, about 2 hours. When you're ready to serve, slice into 16 squares and enjoy!

Pressing the cracker mixture into the pan too hard can result in dense, overly firm treats. Unless that's what you're going for? In which case, your treat.

Tiramisu Pavlova

As someone who finds god in every cup of coffee I drink, I believe this dessert is a love letter to the deep, satisfying flavors and sweet relief that a good brew provides. The crisp Pavlova base, with its marshmallow-like center, serves as the perfect canvas for a rich, espresso-filled topping that pays homage to the beloved Italian classic tiramisu. Topped with a dusting of cocoa powder and dark chocolate shavings, each bite is a celebration of indulgence and sophistication that sings, "That's that me, espresso."

Serves 6 to 8

6 large egg whites, at room temperature

1 cup granulated sugar

1 teaspoon distilled white vinegar

1 teaspoon cornstarch

3 teaspoons pure vanilla extract

1 tablespoon instant espresso powder

2 teaspoons hot water

1½ cups mascarpone cheese, at room temperature

1 cup powdered sugar

1½ cups heavy cream

Unsweetened cocoa powder, for serving

Shaved dark chocolate, for serving

> Don't crack under pressure—some cracks in your Pavlova are totally fine! Sudden temperature changes, however, can cause splits, so let those meringue layers cool inside the oven for a smooth finish.

1   Position racks in the upper and lower thirds of the oven and preheat to 350°F. Line two baking sheets with parchment paper. If you want a precise Pavlova, draw three 6-inch circles in pencil on the parchment (two on one baking sheet and one on the other), then flip the parchment over. Otherwise, you can eyeball it.

2   In a large bowl, whip the egg whites with a handheld mixer on medium speed or by hand with a whisk until opaque and starting to thicken, about 5 minutes. While whipping, gradually add the granulated sugar, then whip until the mixture is glossy, the sugar has fully dissolved, and stiff peaks form, 5 to 6 minutes more. Gently fold in the vinegar, cornstarch, and 1 teaspoon of the vanilla.

3   Spoon the meringue mixture onto the prepared baking sheets, dividing it into three circles (use the pencil circles as guidelines, if you drew them). Transfer to the oven and immediately reduce the oven temperature to 300°F. Bake for about 1 hour, until the Pavlovas are crisp on the outside but still soft inside. Turn off the oven, keeping the oven door closed, and allow the Pavlovas to cool completely, 2 to 3 hours.

4   In a small bowl, stir together the espresso and hot water. Whisk in the mascarpone, powdered sugar, and remaining 2 teaspoons vanilla.

5   In a large bowl, whip the cream with a handheld mixer on medium speed or by hand with a whisk until soft peaks form, about 3 minutes. Add the mascarpone mixture and whip until stiff peaks form, 1 minute more.

6   Just before serving, place one cooled Pavlova layer on a cake stand or serving plate. Top with one-third of the mascarpone cream, then repeat with the remaining Pavlova and mascarpone cream to make two more layers. Dust the top with cocoa powder and sprinkle with chocolate shavings. Slice and serve immediately.

Mango "Sticky" Rice Pudding

In the true spirit of *Scratch That*, this recipe took a turn from its original plan as a semifreddo into a luscious rice pudding. The semifreddo didn't quite pan out, but before freezing, the mixture tasted so good that I knew I had to share it! Rice pudding it is! One of my all-time favorite desserts is mango sticky rice. As a child, I was obsessed with the combo of ripe fruit and creamy coconut milk, and that obsession has carried through into adulthood. This recipe is a tribute to my childhood and love for the flavors of this Thai staple. Here, rich rice pudding meets the bright, sweet, and creamy notes of mango and coconut. I use sushi rice instead of sticky rice for two reasons: It works better in achieving that creamy rice pudding consistency, and frankly, it's easier to find.

1 In a medium saucepan, combine the rice, half the coconut milk, the salt, and 1 cup water. Bring to a boil over medium heat, cover, and reduce the heat to low. Cook, stirring occasionally, until the rice is soft and the water has been absorbed, 15 to 20 minutes. Stir in the remaining coconut milk and the condensed milk. Remove from the heat, cover, and let stand for 15 to 20 minutes, until all the liquid has been absorbed.

2 Fold in the mango. Taste and sweeten with more condensed milk to your liking.

3 Serve warm, or refrigerate until chilled through, about 2 hours. Top with toasted coconut flakes and dig in!

Serves 6 to 8

1 cup sushi rice, rinsed

1 (13.5-ounce) can full-fat coconut milk

½ teaspoon kosher salt

¼ cup sweetened condensed milk, plus more to taste

2 cups thawed frozen diced mango, or 1 (13.5-ounce) can diced mango, drained

Toasted unsweetened coconut flakes, for serving

Use fresh mangoes if they're in season and extra ripe; otherwise, use frozen or canned, which will give more juicy sweetness.

Lemonfetti Bars

I developed this recipe during my last week as a producer at Tasty. Leaving a job that felt like my whole identity was terrifying, and arguably the biggest leap I've taken in my life thus far. Everything felt uncertain. It's funny how such a fun and sweet recipe was born out of such a bittersweet moment, but this vibrant concoction echoes my desire to infuse a bit of joy into my life . . . or should I say to turn lemons into LEMON BARS. The zesty burst of lemon is complemented by the whimsical charm of rainbow sprinkles, and I just can't help but smile at a dessert that mirrors the colorful mosaic of good memories. It's a beautiful reminder that even the saddest goodbyes create room for sweet hellos and new adventures.

Makes 12 bars

Crust

2 cups plus 2 tablespoons all-purpose flour

1 cup (2 sticks) unsalted butter, melted and cooled

½ cup granulated sugar

¼ cup rainbow sprinkles

2 teaspoons pure vanilla extract

½ teaspoon kosher salt

Lemon Filling

2 cups granulated sugar

1 cup fresh lemon juice (from about 7 lemons)

6 large eggs

6 tablespoons all-purpose flour

Rainbow sprinkles (as many as you like!)

Powdered sugar, for dusting

Powdered sugar will melt on a hot surface, so don't rush the sprinkle! Let your lemon bars (or any baked good) cool completely before dusting, or your sugary snow will turn to slush.

1 Preheat the oven to 325°F. Line a 9 × 13-inch glass baking dish with parchment paper, leaving some overhanging the long sides.

2 **Make the crust.** In a medium bowl, stir together the flour, melted butter, granulated sugar, sprinkles, vanilla, and salt. Press the dough into the prepared baking dish in an even layer.

3 Bake the crust for 20 to 25 minutes, until just brown on the edges.

4 **Meanwhile, make the lemon filling.** In a medium bowl, whisk together the granulated sugar, lemon juice, eggs, and flour until smooth.

5 Pour the filling over the hot baked crust and bake for 20 to 25 minutes more, until the filling is set and no longer jiggles. Scatter as many sprinkles as you like across the top of the hot filling, so they set into the top as it cools. Transfer the pan to a wire rack and let cool completely, 2 to 3 hours.

6 Just before serving, dust the bars with powdered sugar. Slice into 12 bars and enjoy!

Cookies & Crème Brûlée

I ate so much crème brûlée as a kid that throughout my twenties, I could barely stand the sight of it. Despite that, this version was one of my earliest recipe videos at Tasty. I take a lot of inspiration from my childhood; I believe it's where our best ideas come from. I combined two well-loved and nostalgic flavors that just so happen to fit perfectly together in the title. I used the cream filling to create the most luxurious custard, its richness perfectly juxtaposed by the playfulness of crushed-up chocolate cookie crumbs. If you're torching the brûlée, use whatever ramekins you have and fill them equally. If you're broiling them, you want to fill the ramekins to the top so the sugar is as close to the heating element as possible—if you only fill them halfway and your broiler is on the weaker side, you may have to leave them under the broiler so long that the custard will heat up and split before the sugar is caramelized. We don't want that! This should be a cookies-and-crème *dream*.

Serves 5 to 10

16 Oreos

4 cups heavy cream

2 teaspoons pure vanilla extract

6 large egg yolks

½ cup sugar, plus more for serving

Boiling water, for the pan

HOT TIP

Tempering is temperamental. We need to gradually bring up the temperature of the eggs so they don't end up scrambled. Slowly add a small amount of hot cream to the eggs while whisking continuously, or else your crème brûlée will end up a breakfast brûlée.

1 Position a rack in the center of the oven and preheat to 300°F. Arrange five 8-ounce, seven 6-ounce, or ten 4-ounce ramekins in a baking dish (or two, if necessary), spacing them apart slightly.

2 Separate the Oreos by twisting them apart. Scrape the filling into a medium saucepan and place the cookies in a quart-size resealable plastic bag. Add the cream to the saucepan and cook over medium heat, whisking continuously, until the filling has melted and the mixture is just about to boil, 8 to 10 minutes. Add the vanilla and remove from the heat. Cover to keep warm.

3 In a large bowl, whisk together the egg yolks and sugar. While whisking continuously, very slowly add the hot cream mixture until everything is incorporated (see Hot Tip). Divide the mixture evenly among the ramekins, filling them.

4 Crush the cookies in the bag into coarse crumbs. Sprinkle 1 tablespoon of the cookie crumbs over each ramekin and stir once just to swirl them in. Carefully transfer the baking dish to the oven, then fill with boiling water so it comes 1 inch up the sides of the ramekins. Bake for about 45 minutes, until the centers are set and no longer jiggly. Remove the ramekins from the water bath and transfer to a wire rack to cool to room temperature, 1 to 2 hours.

5 Cover the ramekins with plastic wrap and gently press it so it touches the custard. Refrigerate for at least 2 hours or up to 24 hours to set.

6 Just before serving, position an oven rack about 6 inches from the broiler heat source and preheat the broiler. Place the ramekins on a baking sheet and sprinkle 1 tablespoon sugar over the top of each. Shake each ramekin to spread the sugar into an even layer. Broil for a few minutes, until the sugar melts and caramelizes. Every broiler is different, so watch closely to prevent burning. (Alternatively, caramelize the sugar on each custard with a kitchen torch.)

7 Crack the tops with a spoon and enjoy!

Chocolate Fudge Cobbler

I guess when it comes to chocolate desserts, I'm either all in or all out, because this one is over the top. This chocolate fudge cobbler is a chocolate lover's—and even liker's!—dream. Better than a brownie, as gooey as a lava cake, and the most decadent decadent can get, it's the only chocolate recipe you'll ever need (don't tell the other chocolate recipes I said that). Best of all, it's a dump-and-bake situation, so you'll have fewer dishes to wash—that's the sweetest treat of all.

Serves 6 to 8

Unsalted butter, for greasing

Brownie Batter

2 cups all-purpose flour

½ cup unsweetened cocoa powder

2 teaspoons baking powder

½ teaspoon kosher salt

1 cup whole milk

¾ cup granulated sugar

4 tablespoons (½ stick) unsalted butter, melted

2 teaspoons pure vanilla extract

Topping

½ cup packed light brown sugar

½ cup granulated sugar

¼ cup unsweetened cocoa powder

4 tablespoons (½ stick) unsalted butter, cubed

2½ cups boiling water

Vanilla ice cream or whipped cream, for serving

1   Preheat the oven to 350°F. Grease an 8-inch square baking dish with butter.

2   **Make the brownie batter.** In the prepared baking dish, whisk together the flour, cocoa powder, baking powder, and salt. Stir in the milk, granulated sugar, melted butter, and vanilla until smooth (be sure there aren't any pockets of the dry ingredients in the corners). It will be very thick—that's what we want. Spread the batter evenly in the baking dish and set the baking dish on a baking sheet.

3   **Make the topping.** In a medium bowl, whisk together the brown sugar, granulated sugar, and cocoa powder. Add the butter and, using your fingers, pinch it into the mixture until coarse, sandlike crumbs form. Sprinkle the mixture over the brownie batter. Pour the boiling water over the top, but do not stir.

4   Bake for 35 to 40 minutes, until the gooey interior is bubbling and the top is crinkled. Remove from the oven and let cool for 15 to 20 minutes. Serve warm, topped with a scoop of vanilla ice cream or a dollop of whipped cream (or both!).

This is neither a cake nor a brownie, so follow the directions closely. The water on top will help form the fudgy sauce underneath the topping. If the fudge is too loose, bake for an extra 7 to 10 minutes.

Milk Chocolate Hazelnut Mousse
WITH HAZELNUT TOFFEE CRUNCH

I've talked some trash on chocolate, and now I feel the need to clarify. I don't love chocolate desserts because they typically lean dark and serious, and I, as a person, am neither of those things. Something happens as you age, and society convinces you the only acceptable chocolate to eat is of the dark variety. I, however, unabashedly adore the mellow, creamy notes of milk chocolate, and this dessert is a rallying cry for my fellow milk enthusiasts. Here it is paired with the delightful nuttiness of hazelnuts and buttery toffee, making this a dessert so good, you might just reconsider your allegiance to the dark side.

Serves 6

1 pound milk chocolate, coarsely chopped

3 cups heavy cream

¼ cup powdered sugar

2 teaspoons pure vanilla extract

1½ cups hazelnuts

½ cup granulated sugar

½ cup (1 stick) unsalted butter

1 Fill a small saucepan with about 1 inch of water and set a heatproof bowl on top; the bowl should not touch the water (see Hot Tip, page 260). Place the chocolate in the bowl and bring the water to a simmer over medium-high heat, stirring the chocolate occasionally. Cook until the chocolate is melted and smooth, about 8 minutes. (Alternatively, melt the chocolate in the microwave in 15-second bursts, stirring after each.) Remove from the heat and let the melted chocolate cool slightly.

2 In a large bowl, combine 2 cups of the cream, the powdered sugar, and 1 teaspoon of the vanilla. Whip with a handheld mixer on medium speed or by hand until soft peaks form (meaning when you stop mixing and pull out the beaters or whisk, the whipped cream forms a "mountain peak" but the top falls over), about 3 minutes, or longer by hand. Gradually fold the melted chocolate into the whipped cream until just combined—do not overmix.

3 Scoop the mousse into six serving glasses or ramekins, dividing it evenly, or into a large serving bowl and smooth out the top. Cover with plastic wrap and gently press it so it touches the mousse. Refrigerate for at least 4 hours or up to 24 hours to set.

4 Meanwhile, preheat the oven to 350°F.

5 Spread the hazelnuts over a baking sheet and toast them in the oven for 10 to 12 minutes, stirring halfway through, until fragrant and lightly golden. Remove and let cool slightly. When they are cool enough to handle, rub the hazelnuts with a clean kitchen towel to remove their skins, then coarsely chop the nuts.

Double boiling prevents direct heat from scorching the chocolate or making it grainy, ensuring a smooth and creamy mousse. The bottom of the bowl should not touch the water; instead, the steam provides the heat. Stir occasionally to melt the chocolate evenly.

6   Line a baking sheet with parchment paper. In a small nonstick skillet, combine the granulated sugar, butter, and ¼ cup water. Cook over medium heat, swirling the pan occasionally (but not stirring), until the sugar is caramelized and deep golden brown, about 12 minutes. Add the hazelnuts and stir to coat. Pour the toffee mixture onto the prepared baking sheet and spread it into an even layer. Set aside to cool and harden completely, about 1 hour, then break or crush the toffee into small pieces.

7   When ready to serve, in a medium bowl, combine the remaining 1 cup cream and 1 teaspoon vanilla and whip with a handheld mixer on medium speed or by hand until soft peaks form, about 2 minutes. Top the chilled mousse with the whipped cream and finish with the toffee crunch.

Roasted Strawberry Cloud Cheesecake

When it comes to dessert preferences, fruit always takes the cake for me—or in this case, the cheesecake. Lest any of my recipes be too straightforward, I thought I'd create a cheesecake of the soufflé variety, which is a hybrid of two great desserts. Instead of being dense, this cheesecake is delightfully airy, thanks to whipped egg whites that give it that FLOOF. The strawberries don't just lend their tartness and sweetness; they also contribute a beautiful pink hue, making this a dessert that's as luscious as it is cute. Light and fluffy, just like a cloud, it's a little slice of heaven on your plate!

Serves 8 to 10

Vegetable oil, for greasing

1 pound fresh strawberries, hulled and halved, plus more for serving (optional)

¾ cup plus 2 tablespoons granulated sugar, plus more as needed

2 tablespoons fresh lemon juice, plus more as needed

Kosher salt

1 (8-ounce) block cream cheese, at room temperature

4 tablespoons (½ stick) unsalted butter, at room temperature

¼ cup all-purpose flour

¼ cup cornstarch

1 tablespoon lemon zest

2 teaspoons pure vanilla extract

4 large egg whites

1 cup heavy cream

Powdered sugar, for serving

Fresh mint leaves, for serving (optional)

1 Preheat the oven to 375°F. Line the bottom of a 9-inch springform pan with parchment paper cut to fit and lightly grease the sides of the pan with oil. Line a baking sheet with parchment.

2 Place the strawberries on the prepared baking sheet. Sprinkle them with ¼ cup of the granulated sugar, 1 tablespoon of the lemon juice, and a pinch of salt. Toss to coat evenly. Taste and adjust with more lemon juice and/or sugar to your liking—they should be pleasantly sweet-tart.

3 Roast the strawberries for 20 to 25 minutes, until they are soft and release some of their juices. Remove from the oven and let cool slightly. Transfer the roasted strawberries and any collected liquid to a blender or food processor and puree on medium-high speed until smooth, about 30 seconds. Measure out 1 cup of the pureed strawberries for the cheesecake, reserving the remainder for serving.

4 Meanwhile, in a large bowl, beat together the cream cheese and butter using a handheld mixer on medium speed or a spatula until smooth and creamy, about 2 minutes. Gradually add the pureed strawberries, mixing to combine well.

5 In a medium bowl, sift together the flour and cornstarch. Gradually add the flour mixture to the cream cheese mixture, mixing with a spatula until smooth. Add the lemon zest, the remaining 1 tablespoon lemon juice, and 1 teaspoon of the vanilla and stir to combine.

6 In a large bowl, whip the egg whites with a handheld mixer on medium speed or by hand until soft peaks form (meaning when you stop mixing and pull out the beaters or whisk, the egg whites form a "mountain peak" but the top falls over), about 3 minutes, or longer by hand.

Soft peaks are light and airy; they gently fold over when you lift out your beaters or whisk. Stiff peaks are sturdy and stable; they stand straight up and hold their shape firmly when you lift out your beaters or whisk. Congrats, you've peaked!

Gradually add ½ cup of the granulated sugar to the egg whites and whip until stiff peaks form (now the peak stays standing!), 2 to 3 minutes more, or longer by hand.

7 In three additions, gently fold the whipped egg whites into the cream cheese mixture until no streaks remain. Pour the batter into the prepared springform pan and smooth out the top. Place the cake pan in a larger baking dish and place it in the oven. Carefully fill the larger pan with enough hot water to come 1 inch up the sides of the cake pan.

8 Bake the cheesecake for 20 minutes, then reduce the oven temperature to 325°F and bake for 30 to 40 minutes more, until the top is lightly golden and the center is set but still slightly jiggly. Turn off the oven and crack open the oven door slightly. Let the cheesecake cool in the oven for 1 hour.

9 Meanwhile, in a large bowl, combine the cream, remaining 2 tablespoons granulated sugar, and remaining 1 teaspoon vanilla. Whip with a handheld mixer on medium speed or by hand until soft peaks form, 2 to 3 minutes. Refrigerate until ready to serve.

10 Remove the cheesecake from the oven; if it's still hot, let it cool until just warm to the touch. Carefully remove the pan from the water bath, then release the sides of the pan. Dust the cheesecake with powdered sugar and top with the whipped cream and any leftover strawberry puree. Serve with fresh strawberries and mint, if desired. Enjoy the same day!

ACKNOWLEDGMENTS

They say it takes a village to raise a child, and the same holds true for writing a cookbook. Time to shoutout those who have helped bring *Scratch That* to life.

Amanda Englander, my brilliant editor: Thank you for taking a chance on my wild, wacky ideas and, most of all, for embracing the mess. **Ivy McFadden**, your insightful feedback and sharp eye helped shape this manuscript into its best form. **Renée Bollier**, your playful vision and design creativity brought this cookbook to life, making each page a joy to turn. **Union Square & Co.**, thank you for bringing my words and vision to life, from "Hot Mess" to "Scratch That." Your tireless work has turned a dream into a tangible reality.

Nicole Tourtelot, my fearless book agent: You wrangled me at just the right time and believed in me long before I believed in myself. Thank for pushing me to use my voice and trust my gut. **Emily Stephenson,** I seriously couldn't have done this thing without you! Like literally, the book would not be done right now because I'd be a year behind. I owe this book's completion to your dedication. **Monique Carlson**, you're the best recipe tester and taster. Thank you for making your way through each recipe with so much care and leaving them better than you found them.

Byron Ashley & **Amanda Hennessy**, I sincerely thank you for your years of hard work and support. I will always cherish our growth and accomplishments together.

Kristin Teig, your keen eye and expertise behind the camera made each dish sing. The photos are the heart of this book. **Marian Cooper-Cairns**, with every spill, splatter, drink fizz, egg yolk drip, you didn't just make the food look good; you made it come alive. **Natalie Drobny**, an absolute BEAST! I was in awe of you churning out dish after dish with such ease and precision. **Jaclyn Kershek**, you didn't just style—you brought color and pizzazz that made every recipe pop. **Ty Ferg**, thank you for making me and every dish glow in ways only the gods can. SLAY. **Noah Swimmer** & **Linnea Toney**, for jumping on this ride with me without hesitation and showing up for this cookbook without expectation.

Mia Gahne, thank you for instilling in me a confidence that has propelled me to where I am today. To my **Tasty fam**, thank you for the laughter, the hustle, and the countless memories. Those lessons, skills, and viral videos are woven into every page.

My beautiful friends, thank you for being my cheerleaders, taste-testers, and critics when necessary (not just of the food!). **Sydney Surprise**, my twin & lover of B. From eating food to wearing food, so much of you is in this book!

Soheila, **Abbas**, **Poya** & **Soudy**, thank you for welcoming me into your family with open hearts and accepting me at the table as SHEEKAMOO! **Mom**, thank you for your wisdom, laughter, and curious spirit and for dancing to ABBA with me in our kitchen, even if it ended with flour in your eye! **Dad**, from one producer to another, thank you for paving the way and always being my greatest champion. **Jeff**, the best big brother, my forever eating partner. **Janna**, I'll forever look up to you for your wit, sass, and huge . . . heart. **Zander**, the most photogenic teddy bear—I mean, dog. Your enthusiasm for eating is unmatched.

Zoya, my love, thank you for being my rock whenever my confidence wavered. You've given me the most precious gift of all—my sense of worth. I love doing life (and food!) with you.

And finally, **my incredible followers**, who feel more like family than fans—thank you for watching my journey unfold and sharing every moment with me. Your unending support, love, and passion for food have been the driving force behind my career and this cookbook. You've made my dreams come true, and I am endlessly grateful for you.

INDEX

Note: Page references in *italic* indicate photographs.

T